P9-CDU-240

GirlScoutsRV.org
800-845-0787

girl scouts
river valleys

This book was generously donated by
**Girl Scouts of Minnesota and
Wisconsin River Valleys**: where
we build girls of courage, confidence
and character (and have lots of fun, too).

Girl Scout Song Book
GIRL SCOUTS, INC.
GIRL SCOUTS
NATIONAL EQUIPMENT
570 LEXINGTON AVE
REPORT for 1933
Who are the Girl Scouts
1912
TWENTY-FIVE YEARS OF GIRL SCOUTING
1937
BY KATHARINE O. WRIGHT
TRUPE
A GIRL SCOUT GAME
SILVER ANNIVERSARY DINNER
DAVIS

includes a letter from

First Lady Michelle Obama

GIRL SCOUTS

A
Celebration of

100

Trailblazing
Years

Betty Christiansen

CANCEL

STEWART, TABORI & CHANG   NEW YORK

contents

includes a letter from

First Lady Michelle Obama

GIRL SCOUTS

A
Celebration of

Trailblazing
Years

Betty Christiansen

STEWART, TABORI & CHANG   NEW YORK

contents

The responsibility of building our future will soon fall to the next generation—making wise choices for their health and well-being, finding the self-confidence and courage to stand up for what they believe in, and working side by side with others to improve the world around them.

As a mother of two daughters, I know how important it is to provide young women with the tools they need to realize their full potential, and that is what Girl Scouts of the USA has aimed to do since its founding a century ago. Since 1912, Girl Scouts has been a positive presence and guiding force for so many American girls. Through field trips, skill-building clinics, service projects, cultural exchanges, and environmental stewardships, Girl Scouting encourages exploration, discovery, and a desire to create positive change.

As we reflect on the past 100 years of Girl Scouting, we also look to a future where every girl is inspired to lead with courage, confidence, and character. I am excited to help celebrate this landmark event, and I am eager to see how the next generation of Girl Scouts will change our world.

Michelle Obama

Michelle Obama
First Lady of the United States
Honorary President of Girl Scouts of the USA

LEFT
Juliette Low sits at her desk at National Headquarters in New York City, 1915.

OPPOSITE
Juliette Low in uniform wearing the Thanks Badge, 1920s

introduction

"I've got something for the girls of Savannah, and all America, and all the world, and we're going to start it tonight!" When those words were spoken by Juliette Gordon Low in 1912, the lives of American girls were changed forever.

Eighteen girls were invited to that very first Girl Scout meeting, held on March 12, 1912. Today, that number has grown to 3.3 million members. In Girl Scouts' first century, millions of girls and women have been Girl Scouts and have held strong to the Promise and Law, whose principles have guided this movement for decades.

Juliette Low firmly believed that American girls needed to live active lives outside the home, where they could contribute to society as full citizens. She knew that encouraging diversity would make Girl Scouting a richer and more embracing experience, one that would allow every girl to blossom. She felt passionately that Girl Scouts should be available to all girls, regardless of race, ethnicity, and socioeconomic status, and that no disability should prevent girls from enjoying opportunities and reaching their full potential.

Juliette Low—and every volunteer and staff person who has followed in her footsteps during the last 100 years—has held true to that vision while offering a clear and powerful message to every girl: *You matter.*

You matter to your Girl Scout friends. You matter to your community. You matter to the nation. You matter to the world.

OPPOSITE
Girl Scouts on the Observation Post for Signalers at Camp Lowlands,
Savannah, Georgia, circa 1914–1917

BELOW
Early Girl Scouts carry bedrolls over their shoulders while
backpacking, 1917.

BOTTOM
Girl Scouts on their mark before a footrace, 1912

OPPOSITE ABOVE
Carnation Girl Scout Patrol championship basketball team, 1912

OPPOSITE BELOW
White Rose Girl Scout Patrol at naturalist W. J. Hoxie's cabin, Camp
Lowlands, Georgia, circa 1910s

BELOW
A 1936 memo from Savannah documents the first meeting, in 1912,
of Girl Guides in America.

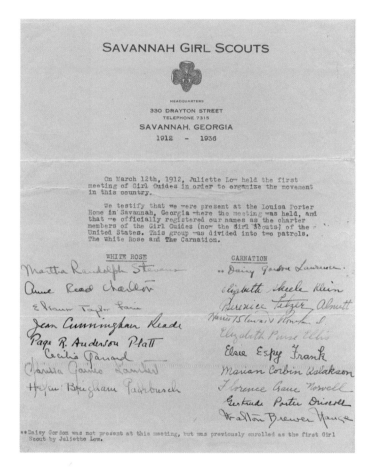

Even more important, Girl Scouting shows girls
that they matter by giving them the opportunity to be
leaders, both today and in the future.

During the past 100 years, Girl Scouts has made
improving the lives of girls—and inspiring girls to
improve the world around them—its singular mission.
Many of today's female role models—including former
Supreme Court justice Sandra Day O'Connor, NASA
astronaut Mae Jemison, TV journalists Barbara
Walters and Katie Couric, former secretary of labor
Alexis Herman, actresses America Ferrera and Reese
Witherspoon, women's rights activist Gloria Steinem,
fashion designer Vera Wang, champion golfer Nancy
Lopez, and racecar driver Danica Patrick—are Girl
Scouts who attribute their determination, integrity,
and achievement to that experience.

Today, we are poised to move into our second
century. The same energy that inspired Juliette Low
in 1912 continues today and will continue for decades
to come. Inspired by our mission—to build girls of
courage, confidence, and character who make the
world a better place—we will not stop until our job
is done and all girls can see a future filled with hope,
opportunity, and achievement.

Connie L. Lindsey
National President
Girl Scouts of the USA

Kathy Cloninger
National Chief Executive Officer
Girl Scouts of the USA

1912–1919

Something for the Girls of America

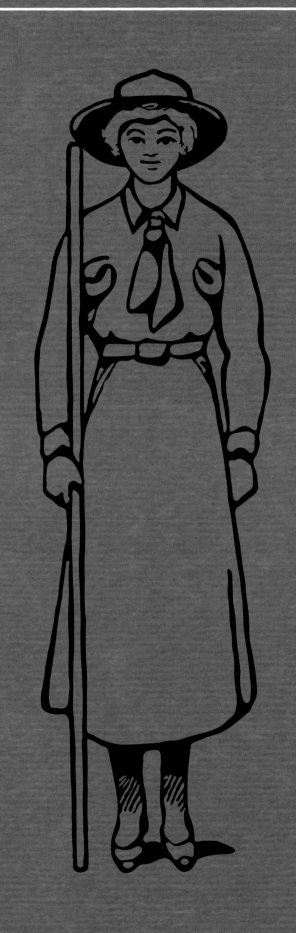

The world in 1912 was on the cusp of change that would rock the foundations of American society for generations to come, for better and for worse. American women were mobilizing forces all over the country to acquire the right to vote. Henry Ford was about to revolutionize manufacturing with assembly-line production of the Model T, and as the world mourned the sinking of the *Titanic*, hearts soared with a pilot named Harriet Quimby, who became the first woman to fly across the English Channel.

Amid these events of 1912 was one that would affect the lives of millions of American girls and women for generations: Juliette Gordon Low, a 51-year-old Savannah native and world traveler, finally discovered her true life's work and founded Girl Scouts of the USA, and in doing so launched one of the most impressive, enduring, and respected movements in recorded history.

Juliette Magill Kinzie Gordon was born in Savannah, Georgia, on October 31, 1860. Her parents, William Washington Gordon II and Eleanor Kinzie Gordon, were members of prominent families and gave their six children every advantage they could. W. W. Gordon was a successful businessman, cotton factor, legislator, humanitarian, and natural leader who fought in the Civil War as a Confederate officer and in the Spanish-American War as a general in the United States Volunteer Army. Nelly Gordon was feisty, charming, and artistic. She wrote several books, including one about her famous grandfather,

Patriotism

During World War I, Girl Scouts demonstrated their now famous ability to mobilize around a cause, effecting change on a grand scale. Girl Scouts were active participants in the Wake Up, America rally and other Liberty Loan drives. They sold U.S. Treasury bonds, spread the word about ways to conserve food and observe rationing laws, rolled bandages, sold cookies to raise money (a nod toward future endeavors), and collected peach pits on a national scale to be used in gas mask filters. The far-reaching patriotism of Girl Scouts not only served the country in a time of need but also led to a surge in membership and increased national exposure.

SIDEBAR
Girl Scouts at a flag ceremony support their country by selling Liberty Bonds, 1918.

BELOW
As a child, Johnny Mercer, a famous American composer and lyricist, allowed Girl Scouts to practice their first aid on him in exchange for a "co-cola," 1913.

BOTTOM
Girl Scouts team up to preserve fruits and vegetables in response to food shortages, circa 1917.

John Kinzie, a founder of the city of Chicago. Juliette Gordon, their second child, became a strong-minded leader in her own large family, an independent spirit who from a young age challenged conventional ideas about what a girl should do.

Juliette Gordon—known as "Daisy" to her friends and family—enjoyed a childhood filled with imagination and independence. She spent several summers with her siblings and cousins at her aunt's home at Etowah Cliffs in northern Georgia. There, she wrote poems, stories, and plays with roles for all the children (saving the best roles for herself) and developed a lifelong passion for studio arts, especially painting, drawing, and sculpting. During these idyllic summers, Daisy and her playmates thoroughly explored their outdoor surroundings. They swam, climbed trees, organized make-believe games, and embarked on imaginary hunting expeditions. Daisy also loved animals, and throughout her life she always had at least one dog, as well as exotic birds and other pets.

In her teenage years, Daisy was sent to boarding schools in Virginia and New Jersey, including the Virginia Female Institute, which is now called Stuart Hall School, and later to a French finishing school in New York City.

Having completed her schooling, Daisy turned her interest to traveling abroad. Eventually, she spent most of each year living in England and Scotland. It was during one such stay in England that she renewed her acquaintance with a distant cousin, William Mackay Low, whose father maintained business interests and a home in Savannah. They married in 1886, against the wishes of her father, who considered William Low irresponsible and hoped Daisy would make a more sensible choice. Billow, as Daisy called her husband, was a man who lived large, mingling with royalty and aristocracy, and entertaining high-society friends at his English and Scottish estates.

Sadly, their marriage began to disintegrate. Unhappy in her marriage and feeling a deep desire to make her own impact on the world, Daisy embarked on a quest for her own life's purpose. She also continued her travels back and forth to the United States, where she threw herself into selfless work, including helping her mother organize a convalescent hospital for wounded soldiers returning from Cuba during the Spanish-American War.

Her husband was pressing for a divorce when he died suddenly in 1905 after an extended period of failing health. When his estate was finally settled, Juliette Low found herself, at age 45, financially secure and just as rich in friends and family, but still feeling aimless and fearing she was living a "wasted life." Always filled with youthful energy and much adored by her nieces and nephews, she was deeply disappointed that she'd never had children of her own. She continued to divide her time between England and the United States, travel the world, and pursue her art, yet she yearned for a higher purpose and referred to herself as "an idle woman of the world with no real work or duties."

That ended in 1911 when, in London, she made the acquaintance of Sir Robert Baden-Powell, a war hero, leader in the British "youth movement," and founder of the Boy Scouts and Girl Guides in Britain. Baden-Powell introduced her to his sister, Agnes, who led the Girl Guides. Juliette Low became active with Girl Guide troops in London and Scotland, and became increasingly inspired by and excited about that movement, whose mission to foster a sense of citizenship and camaraderie in young people struck a true chord with her. Before long, her life's purpose became clear to her, and she decided to bring the movement home to America. Back in Savannah, in early March 1912, she made a phone call that was to change American girlhood, exclaiming to her cousin, Nina Pape, "Come right over! I've got something for the girls of Savannah, and all America, and all the world, and we're going to start it tonight."

Just a few days later, on March 12, Juliette Low officially signed up 18 girls, who formed two small patrols, the very first American Girl Guides. Her niece and namesake, Daisy "Doots" Gordon, was the first registered member. The girls, all 12 or older, gathered in Juliette Low's carriage house for meetings; donned blue uniforms; and focused on careers, nature, first aid, and team sports such as basketball. Juliette Low also purchased land near Savannah for a campsite she named Lowlands, at which girls could explore nature and learn outdoor skills. In 1913, the name of her organization was changed to Girl Scouts, and an American icon was born.

BELOW

Across from Savannah's Andrew Low House, in 1914, a Girl Scout
shoots a hoop during a basketball game as others look on. The fence
shields the girls in their athletic clothing.

BOTTOM

Packed and ready for camp, young Girl Scouts pose in front of
Savannah's Girl Scout Headquarters, circa 1913.

The Golden Eaglet

The 1918 silent film *The Golden Eaglet* is a movie every Girl Scout should see, as well as an inspiring and groundbreaking contribution to American cinematic history. Watching it, viewers follow the adventures of Margaret Ferris as she forms a Girl Scout troop, communicates using semaphore and Morse code, rescues a railroad master, and cares for a soldier's family on her way to earning the Golden Eaglet, the highest award in Girl Scouting at that time.

SIDEBAR LEFT
In this still from *The Golden Eaglet*, the Girl Scout heroine Margaret uses her knowledge of Morse code to get help for a hurt station manager.

SIDEBAR RIGHT
In the film, Juliette Low pins Margaret with the Golden Eaglet.

SIDEBAR BOTTOM
Filming *The Golden Eaglet*, 1918

BELOW

The first Girl Scout handbook, *How Girls Can Help Their Country*, was published in 1913.

SIDEBAR TOP TO BOTTOM

Girl Scout proficiency badges, 1913–1918: Artist, Child Nurse, Naturalist

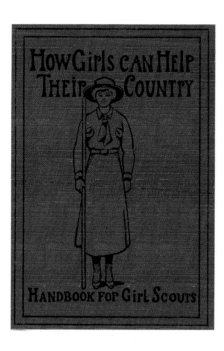

Juliette Low had brought back with her from London a copy of the British Girl Guide handbook, *How Girls Can Help to Build Up the Empire*, and a handful of badges. She enlisted the naturalist Walter John Hoxie to adapt the manual for an American audience, resulting in *How Girls Can Help Their Country*. Published in 1913, the handbook was full of forward-thinking concepts about girls and was fairly radical in encouraging girls to master a trade, or even two trades, so that they could be independent. Filled with descriptions of proficiency badges encouraging girls to explore areas outside the traditional realm of women, the book also suggested that girls learn semaphore and Morse code to ready themselves for emergencies and perform service to their country.

Badges

Proficiency badges were introduced in 1912 and were used to signify accomplishments in various areas. Early badges were offered for categories ranging from Laundress to Artist to Electrician, and the very first were hand-embroidered by Girl Scouts and adult volunteers. The badges represented a wide range of girls' interests and practical skills.

Badges were revised and re-created over the years to reflect accomplishments relevant to the times. For example, badges are still awarded for accomplishments similar to those recognized in 1913—such as Health (now Eating for Beauty) and Needlewoman (now Textile Artist)— but among those you'll also find now are Car Care, Social Innovator, Design, and Science of Happiness.

The Rally

The Girl Scout magazine *The Rally* was launched in 1917. Though it was initially written for Captains (adult volunteers), the audience soon included girls. In 1920, its name was changed from *The Rally* to *The American Girl,* which it was called until publication ceased in 1979. For many years, however, it was the most successful and widely read publication for girls in America.

THE RALLY

Published monthly by
National Headquarters Girl Scouts, Inc.

Vol. I. No. 1   October, 1917   Ten cents a copy / One dollar a year

Captains of their Souls

By JOSEPHINE DASKAM BACON

*"I am the master of my fate,
I am the captain of my soul!"*
—W. E. Henley.

ONE of the greatest tributes to the Girl Scout movement has just been made, in a very simple, matter-of-fact way by the daily press of London.

England, all torn and battered and harassed as she is by the greatest war that ever shook the world, must take time, as all warring nations must take time, to consider the effect of this war upon the most important part of any community—its young people. And London is finding among her young people a growing unrest and a dangerous tendency toward escape from the ordinary restraints.

If you will think for a moment, you will see how natural and inevitable this is. Every day, every hour, the men and women who occupy their business or their leisure time with the direction, the training or the entertainment of young people are being thrown into more pressing war duties. Teachers, clergymen, policemen, nurses, district visitors, Big Brothers and Big Sisters of all sorts are enlisting in the great army which is England; the very mothers themselves must neglect a little their own broods, and sew and cook and nurse for their adopted sons at the Front.

And what is the result?

Lawlessness increases; juvenile crime grows more daring, because there is less time to suppress it; vagrancy, truancy and disobedience are beginning to force themselves upon the notice of the city authorities.

And so we find the authorities meeting to discuss these things. And in the report of their meeting, I read with great interest in a London paper:

"The Council strongly urges an increased activity in the Boy Scout and Girl Guide movements, as most helpful in the present crisis."

Nothing in my opinion, can speak more clearly for the practical value of these movements than this earnest recommendation to hard-headed, practical men. They are not, you

will notice, inventing a new remedy or guessing at results. They are urging an extension of an institution with which they are already well and favorably acquainted. They do not suggest that something like the Girl Guides should be tried, and see what happens—they have seen it tried, and they know what happens, and they want more of it!

Now, the Girl Guides of England are the Girl Scouts of America. If they have been proved to put girls on their honor. to make them trusty, efficient, self-controlled young citizens in war time in England, they will certainly prove these things for England's great Ally.

To me this great fact stands out, wonderfully thrilling and comforting.

Aside from their various technical abilities of knot-tying, semaphoring, first-aiding, cooking, sewing and child-tending, Girl Scouts can be counted upon for self-controlling, self-policing. This recommendation of the London council means, if it means anything, that *every Girl Scout the more means one girl the less for the community to worry about, one girl the more for the neighborhood to rely on!*

Surely, if this is so, the movement cannot spread too rapidly or too thoroughly for the good of a country which is advancing further and further into the great world-contest every day.

Long before we were at war, the Laws of the Girl Scouts began with these:

"A girl scout's honor is to be trusted.
"A girl scout is loyal.
"A girl scout's duty is to be useful and to help others."

They must have lived up to these laws, one feels, to have convinced the government that England needed more of them.

Surely this plain recognition of what we stand for before the world should act as a real

SIDEBAR

The inaugural edition of *The Rally* was published by Girl Scout National Headquarters in October 1917. Its title changed to *The American Girl* in 1920.

OPPOSITE

A troop stands outside Girl Scout National Headquarters in Manhattan, home to the organization from June 1917 to November 1918.

Juliette Low served as the organization's first President, a position she held for five years. She established the National Headquarters in Washington, D.C., in 1913, and then moved it to New York City in 1916, where it is still located today. In 1915, Girl Scouts was officially incorporated, and the organization grew rapidly. Drawing on her worldly knowledge and backed by a cadre of talented volunteers and staff, she recruited a board of directors featuring like-minded, influential women such as Lou Henry Hoover, Jane Deeter Rippin, and Edith Macy, and together they mobilized support nationwide. They rallied women they knew all over the country to establish Girl Scout troops in their areas—from Savannah up the eastern seaboard to Washington, D.C., New York, and Boston, then westward from Chicago to Los Angeles. And women nationwide, eager to promote opportunities for girls, were easily convinced by these charismatic ambassadors.

At the close of 1914, Girl Scouts boasted more than 1,000 members; by 1915, that number had leapt to 5,000. By 1916, more than 7,000 girls had joined the movement. In 1917, the first Girl Scout leaders' training school was established to train these new volunteers, and publications such as the Girl Scout handbook *How Girls Can Help Their Country* offered guidance as well. That same year, the National Equipment Service was established to handle the administration of uniforms, insignia, and other items through catalog sales, and this became a booming, women-run business. Juliette Low had accomplished

Inclusivity

Juliette Low firmly believed that *every* girl should be able to become a Girl Scout, and it went without saying that diversity and respect for differences were important aspects of the Girl Scout program. This philosophy stemmed from not only her own lifelong convictions but also a personal experience with disability—she had lost most of her hearing by her mid-20s.

From the very beginning, the movement took pride in its efforts to make Girl Scouts available to girls of all abilities and also all races, religions, income levels, geographic locations, and nationalities. Decades before the civil rights movement, African American girls were active Girl Scouts; despite immigration controversies, Hispanic and Asian girls earned badges and joined troops all over the country. Since 1912, Girl Scouts has welcomed with open arms any girl willing to live up to the ideals of the Girl Scout Promise and Girl Scout Law.

SIDEBAR
A Girl Scout who is blind reads from a braille handbook.

BELOW
The cover of the first *Girl Scout Equipment,* April 1917, shows where to place uniform insignia.

BOTTOM
Members of the Lily of the Valley Patrol Basketball Team pose for a portrait in Savannah, Georgia, 1913.

During 1935's Girl Scout Week, Mrs. Woodrow Wilson visits the national Little House to view arts-and-crafts displays made by Girl Scouts at camp. Girl Scouts greet her with the "pass and review" formation.

her dream in true Girl Scout fashion: through a combination of enthusiasm, charisma, perseverance, and hard work.

As Girl Scouts continued to grow, so did its opportunity to make a nationwide impact. Girl Scouts' pledged commitment to service and duty to country was called up in countless ways during World War I as girls across the country threw themselves into the war effort, taking up efforts that ranged from planting Victory Gardens to selling war bonds. In fact, Girl Scouts' war bond sales over the course of World War I topped $9 million; in recognition, the U.S. Treasury in 1918 struck the Girl Scout Liberty Loan Medal in bronze.

Accomplishments such as this attracted no small amount of attention for Girl Scouts, leading more and more girls to join. But with this growth came inevitable changes. For many years, for example, Juliette Low invested a substantial portion of her own fortune to ensure that Girl Scouts remained successful. As Girl Scouts continued to attract members, her personal finances could no longer support the rapid expansion. When she began making personal sacrifices to save money—such as selling a prized string of pearls to finance the movement for another year—it became clear that Girl Scouts needed outside support and funding, and outreach on behalf of Girl Scouts began in earnest. In 1915, Juliette Low reluctantly established membership dues of 25 cents a year, and shortly after that the Executive Board inaugurated a plan to raise money for the

First Ladies

In 1917, Juliette Low asked First Lady Edith B. Wilson to become the Honorary National President of Girl Scouts. Since that date, every First Lady has kept the tradition, including Michelle Obama in 2009, who made a statement calling Girl Scouts "a positive force for change—in their own lives, their communities, and across the globe."

Trefoil

Juliette Low patented the design for the original three-leafed membership badge (pin)—the trefoil—on February 10, 1914. Each of the three leaves stands for a part of the Girl Scout Promise, and the design features traditional American symbols: an eagle, a shield, a shaft of arrows, and an olive branch. Girl Scouts still uses a three-leafed trefoil today, although the design was changed in 1978 to feature three forward-looking faces, symbolizing diversity, continuing commitment, and—of course—girls.

SIDEBAR
Official documentation for the original trefoil badge, designed and patented by Juliette Low in 1914

BELOW
A group of adult Girl Scout leaders share books and listen to a presentation about becoming a leader of Girl Scouts at a New York City training camp, 1918.

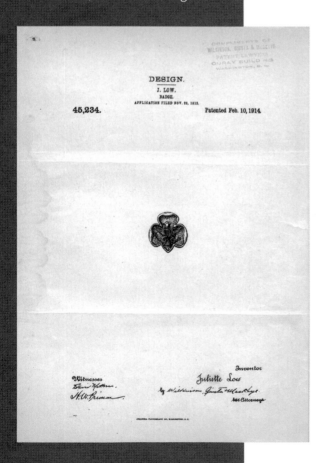

SIDEBAR
Girl Scouting continued to expand as the first troops were formed in
the Hawaiian Islands. Pictured here is one of Hawaii's early Girl Scouts,
circa 1917.

Aloha

In 1917, when Hawaii was not yet a
state, Queen Lili'uokalani (who was
to be the last Hawaiian queen) and
a teacher named Florence Lowe
decided that the islands needed a
Girl Scout troop of their own. The
first Hawaiian Girl Scout troop was
founded in Honolulu in 1917 at the
Kamehameha School for Girls, where
Ms. Lowe taught. Shortly after, another
group of Hawaiian girls from an area
called Kaka'ako formed the second
Hawaiian Girl Scout troop. The original
O'ahu Council was organized in 1918
and first chartered by Girl Scouts in
May of 1919.

Famous Words

THE GIRL SCOUT PROMISE

On my honor, I will try:
To serve God and my country,
To help people at all times,
And to live by the Girl Scout Law.

THE GIRL SCOUT LAW

I will do my best to be

 honest and fair,

 friendly and helpful,

 considerate and caring,

 courageous and strong, and

 responsible for what I say and do,

and to

 respect myself and others,

 respect authority,

 use resources wisely,

 make the world a better place, and

 be a sister to every Girl Scout.

The Girl Scout Promise and Law have been updated throughout the years. The current Promise and Law are listed above.

SIDEBAR
This 1925 rendition of the Girl Scout Promise was designed by illustrator Edith Ballinger Price, who helped develop the Brownie program.

OPPOSITE
Girl Scouts pose with Juliette Low and the "Founder's Banner" in a Savannah yard. The photo was later included in the October 1924 issue of *The American Girl* as part of the Founder's birthday message.

organization. Edith Macy donated the first $1,000 in 1916, and devoted volunteers everywhere continued to offer their commitment of time and enthusiasm. People recognized the potential this young organization had to enhance the lives of thousands more American girls, and they were willing to step up and help.

Their hard work and dedication paid off tremendously. By 1920, there were active Girl Scout troops in each of the 48 states and the territory of Hawaii. Membership has steadily increased in the century since, and while the movement is ever changing to meet the needs of each generation, the key elements of Juliette Low's original vision have never wavered. Girl Scouts still wear uniforms reflecting the styles and needs of the times; they still use a Girl Scout handbook, live the Promise and Law, earn awards and badges, and provide service to others. In eight short years, Juliette Low had transformed a fledgling notion into a movement that has since become a grand and enduring American tradition, and a transformative experience for American girls.

The Girl Scout's Promise

On my Honor I will try
To do my Duty to God and my Country
To help other People at all times
To Obey the Scout Laws

1920s

Eyes on the Future

OPPOSITE
A Girl Scout cares for a baby outside a Manhattan barbershop as a
mother votes, one year after women got the vote.

BELOW
The first issue of *The American Girl,* June 1920

America in the 1920s was a thriving, vibrant, optimistic place to live, particularly for women. They had just gained the right to vote, and their eyes were fixed on freedom and the future. They bobbed their hair, discarded their corsets and relaxed into Coco Chanel's soft and feminine fashions, and enjoyed all the Roaring Twenties had to offer. Women increasingly made their way into the headlines: Transatlantic pilot Amelia Earhart became a national hero, and Mary Pickford dominated silent film as a legendary actress and producer.

Girl Scouts was just as thriving, vibrant, and optimistic, having grown to such an extent—more than 50,000 girls by 1920—that a full-time staff was required to run daily operations and support the many dedicated volunteers. A new handbook, *Scouting for Girls,* was published by the national organization, replacing the original *How Girls Can Help Their Country,* an adaptation of the British Girl Guides handbook. The Girl Scout magazine *The Rally* became *The American Girl,* and within a few years, a leader's supplement to it, *Field News,* developed into its own magazine, *Leader,* offering further support and direction to volunteer leaders across the country.

At the same time that Girl Scouts was growing and changing within the borders of the United States, it also continued its relationship with the global Scouting movement. Sir Robert Baden-Powell, who had inspired Juliette Low's ambitions and led the Boy Scout movement in England, was named the "Chief Scout of the World," and Scouting became firmly established as

SIDEBAR
With the innovation of the Radio Troop, 1928's annual report was titled
Broadcast from Station "Girl Scout" with Television Pictures.

Radio Troops

Ever ahead of their time, a group of Girl Scouts in Pittsburgh formed a Radio Troop in celebration of the newfangled, groundbreaking contraption, with the help of one of the earliest radio stations in the country, KDKA.

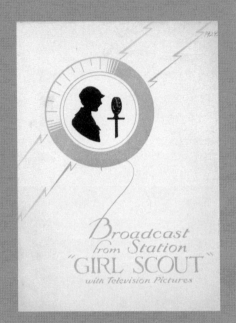

1920s *Eyes on the Future*

36

an international institution. In 1920, the International Council of Girl Guides and Girl Scouts held its first conference in Oxford, England, hosting delegates and visitors from 15 countries.

Closer to home, the first American Indian Girl Scout troop was established on the Onondaga Reservation in Syracuse, New York, in 1921, and a Mexican American troop was formed in Houston, Texas, in 1922. In 1923, Girl Scouts extended its reach into remote pockets of the country through Radio Troop meetings. The Pittsburgh radio station KDKA invited area Girl Scouts to broadcast Girl Scouting to girls across the United States who did not have access to a physical troop. Laura Holland Macdonald, the local director, broadcast the troop's meeting every Monday at 7:00 p.m. Juliette Low's insistence that Girl Scouts be a movement open to *all* American girls, regardless of their differences or location, was thoroughly honored.

Thanks to the generosity of devoted supporters in this decade, Girl Scouts were able to enjoy favorite aspects of Girl Scouting—like camping—on a new level. In 1920, Senator William Clark and his wife, Anna, founded a camp in honor of their daughter Andrée Clark, who was an active Girl Scout member when she died at age 16. Located in Briarcliff Manor, New York, about 45 minutes outside New York City, Camp Andrée Clark was used as a training camp for girls ages 14 and older who were interested in becoming Girl Scout leaders themselves, and the first established camp, held in 1922, was attended by two Girl Scouts from each state.

BELOW LEFT
Girl Scouts examine trees and take notes in the woods as part of
requirements for the new naturalist badge and nature program, which
started around this time, circa 1920s.

BELOW RIGHT
At Camp Juliette Low in Cloudlands, Georgia, pioneering Girl Scouts
build a "Hoover Hut" and practice carpentry skills, 1920.

BOTTOM
A Girl Scout prepares to light a fire at Camp Edith Macy in New York,
circa 1920s.

Examining an exhibit at the Wonder House's Nature Club, 1920

Reading in "The Cave" at California's Camp Chapparal, circa 1920s

A group of Girl Scouts work around a fire at Camp Andrée Clark, 1922.

BELOW
In 1924, a uniformed Juliette Low chats with the American Delegation of Girl Scouts at England's Word Camp at Foxlease.

BOTTOM
As Girl Scouts sleep on the ground at Camp Chapparal in California in 1925, their cloth pocket mess kits hang on a tree behind.

OPPOSITE
A group hikes Lookout Mountain's rocky hillside in Cloudlands, Georgia, circa 1920.

LEFT
The front of this brochure introduces the Little House, a model American home where girls learned domestic skills.

OPPOSITE ABOVE
Girl Scouts decorate the door to the Little House in Washington, D.C., with an evergreen wreath, circa 1920s.

OPPOSITE BELOW
A sitting room in the Little House is furnished in memory of Juliette Low, circa 1920s.

The Girl Scout And Her Little House

❖

Girl Scouts, Inc.
670 Lexington Avenue
New York, N. Y.

The camping craze, however, was not limited to leaders-in-training. The popularity of camping sparked early on at Savannah's Lowlands spread rapidly. In addition to introducing girls of that time to a pastime largely enjoyed by boys, camping fostered independence and teamwork, strength and perseverance, a love of nature, and a sense of camaraderie and sisterhood—all qualities embodied by Juliette Low herself. By 1924, more than 38,000 Girl Scouts attended camp at 304 locations around the country, ensuring that Girl Scouts everywhere—in northern woods and redwood forests, in winter snow and on the seashore—learned to pitch tents and build campfires as handily as they could mend a garment or tidy a house.

Yet those practical domestic skills were not ignored by Girl Scouts—on the contrary, they were studied and sharpened through training stations such as the Little House in Washington, D.C. In this model of an "average" American home, girls were taught useful, daily skills essential for any woman living independently or running a household. The Little House was built and exhibited by the General Federation of Women's Clubs in 1923, then was offered to Girl Scouts, who in 1924 moved it to a permanent location. Used as a national demonstration center until April 1945, it became a national branch office and was used until May 1955.

A permanent home for leadership training was also a particular dream of certain Girl Scout leaders, one of whom was Edith Macy, a Girl Scout National

OPPOSITE
A parade of the national flags of Girl Guides and Girls Scouts from 29 nations, at Camp Edith Macy World Camp, Fourth International Conference, May 1926

RIGHT TOP AND BOTTOM
Invitations to the Fourth International Conference at Camp Edith Macy, 1926

Board member from 1919 to 1925 and a strong supporter of the movement since its earliest years. In 1925, five years after the opening of Camp Andrée Clark and shortly after Edith Macy's death, Camp Edith Macy was established adjacent to Camp Andrée. The land was donated by V. Everit Macy in memory of his wife. From May 11 to May 17, 1926, the camp was host to the Fourth International Conference on Scouting, the first international Girl Scouting event held on American soil, attended by 56 delegates from 31 countries. On the opening evening, Juliette Low dedicated the camp to the memory of Edith Macy.

Camp Edith Macy soon became known as the Girl Scouts' "University in the Woods." Beginning in 1927, it offered one- and two-week classes for adult Girl Scouts who were leaders, council members, or staff. The classes included the latest information about the ever-evolving Girl Scout programs, and students had the opportunity to meet with peers. Across the road, Camp Andrée Clark became the testing ground for many ideas that later found their way into the handbooks. The students lived in one of four outdoor units and gathered in the evenings around communal campfires. Today, Camp Edith Macy continues the tradition of training adults involved in Girl Scouting and is a modern conference center as well.

As Girl Scouts flourished (between 1920 and 1921 alone, membership doubled to more than 112,000), earning money took on new importance. Staff and volunteers alike came to realize the need

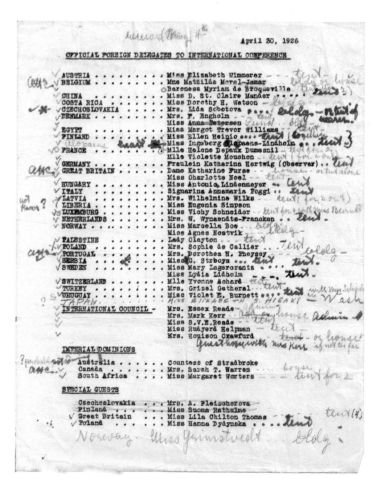

BELOW
Delegates from 29 countries attend the Fourth International
Conference, from May 11 to 17, 1926, at Camp Edith Macy.

OPPOSITE
Music is part of Girl Scout activities and culture, circa 1920s.

GIRL SCOUT WEEK!

MONDAY'S Scout is at the tub,
Her Sunday clothes to rinse and rub.

TUESDAY'S Scout will roast and stew
And fry fresh pancakes just for you!

WEDNESDAY'S Scout is bent on Thrift,
To patch the hole and darn the rift.

THURSDAY is Scout Service Day,
For helping your neighbor in many a way.

FRIDAY'S Scout is rosy and strong,
She camps and "hikes" the whole day long.

SATURDAY'S Scout is happy and gay
For this is Baby Caring Day.

While SUNDAY'S Scout presents to you
Her ununiformed back in the family pew!

EVERY WEEK IS GIRL SCOUT WEEK
Everywhere in the United States and her Territories

Make checks payable to Girl Scouts, Inc.,
189 Lexington Avenue, New York City

WILL YOU GIVE A DAY'S PAY?

for ongoing, widespread efforts to earn money, and this necessity gave rise to a much-loved and much-anticipated Girl Scout tradition: the Girl Scout cookie sale. Although Girl Scouts baked and sold cookies as early as 1917—an Oklahoma Girl Scout troop, for example, held a bake sale in a school cafeteria as a service project that year—Girl Scout cookies didn't hit the national stage until 1922, when Chicago Girl Scout leader Florence E. Neil created a cookie recipe that was distributed to 2,000 local members.

Neil's recipe, published in the July issue of *The American Girl*, was for a simple sugar cookie. She suggested that the cookies be sold for 25 to 30 cents per dozen—approximately the cost of making six to seven dozen cookies—which gave troops a generous profit to use for their activities. Until the mid-1930s, when production was entirely turned over to commercial bakeries and a new chapter in the history of Girl Scout cookies was begun, Girl Scouts nationwide baked cookies using Neil's recipe, packaging them in their home kitchens in waxed paper or brown paper bags, and selling them door-to-door. An exception took place in 1928, when a Girl Scout troop in Paris, Texas, sold 600 dozen cookies baked for them by a local baking company—the earliest known sale of commercially baked Girl Scout cookies.

Another defining icon of Girl Scouts—badges—saw an explosion in the 1920s. A bewildering array of badges was created, discontinued, revived, and changed until a decision was made in 1927 to publish

Original Girl Scout Cookie Recipe

The AMERICAN GIRL

If every Scout of the two thousand in Cook County bakes and sells one batch of cookies every month, the money taken in will amount to $2,000.00 a month of $24,000.00 for the entire year. Think it over. Is there *any* scout who is not willing to do her share?

ATTENTION SCOUTS! FORWARD MARCH! BAKE! SELL!

This is your chance to show how much Scouting means to you.

GIRLS SCOUT COOKIES

1 cup of Butter, or substitute,
1 cup of sugar
2 tablespoons of milk
2 eggs
1 teaspoon of vanilla
2 cups of flour
2 teaspoons of baking powder.

Cream butter and sugar, add well beaten eggs, then milk, flavoring, flour and baking powder. Roll thin and bake in quick oven.

(Sprinkle sugar on top.)

This amount makes six to seven dozen.

The verse below was printed on cards and distributed.

COOKIES large and cookies small,
Made by SCOUTS both short and tall.
What's your ORDER? Phone us quick,
So that we may do the trick.
THIRTY CENTS is all we ask,
And we find it is no task
To DELIVER to your door,
DOZENS—one, two, three—or more!
Telephone

The American Girl, July 1922

Brownies

Soon after Girl Scouts was established, it became clear that younger girls wanted to be involved, too. In 1922, Girl Scouts released a manual, *The Brownie Book*, with experimental material about starting a Brownie program in the United States. After the First American Brownie Pow-Wow was held that same year, Brownie Girl Scouts became the official program for younger girls.

An official leader's manual, *The Brown Book for Brown Owls*, was published in 1926. A pullover brown dress was introduced as the official uniform in 1927.

SIDEBAR BELOW
Girl Scout Brownie Fly-Up Wings, 1927–1935

SIDEBAR BOTTOM
Girl Scout Brownie membership pin, 1921–1937

BELOW FROM TOP TO BOTTOM
Girl Scout proficiency badges, 1920s–1930s: Scholarship, Cook, First Aide, Garden Flower Finder

new badge books once a year and to allow six months for changes to take effect. Badges were created to reflect the world in which girls were living and learning, and the 1920s ushered in recognition of an ever-expanding number of possibilities.

For example, to earn the Economist badge introduced in the 1920s, a Girl Scout had to, among other qualifications, establish a savings account, use her allowance to buy durable, high-quality stockings, and mend torn or worn clothing before carelessly replacing it with new items. (Today, a badge called Financing My Future requires girls to research financial aid and scholarship options for their educational dreams.) Many badges were modernized in this era; for example, the Automobiling badge, introduced in 1918, was renamed Motorist in 1920, while Clerk became Business Woman.

At the same time that Girl Scouts was focusing on creating new opportunities for the girls already in its ranks, it also began to reach out to girls of younger ages. Since 1914, a program called Rosebuds had existed in England, an extension of Girl Guides designed to accommodate tagalong younger sisters. Sir Robert Baden-Powell changed the name to Brownies, inspired by the brownie elves of English folklore, little fairy creatures who lived in humans' homes and did good deeds. The idea took root in the United States, where a Girl Scout Brownie troop, or "pack," was organized in Massachusetts as early as 1916, but it was not until the 1920s that the national organization determined what, precisely, the Brownies

Girl Scout Brownies sing with a smile, circa 1920s.

were going to be. In 1921, an issue of *The American Girl* addressed the early concept, explaining that Brownies offered "suitable, age-appropriate activities for girls too young to be Girl Scouts." By the end of that year, Brownie packs consisting of girls ages 7 to 10 were established in seven states, ranging from New Jersey to Oregon. In 1922, *The Brownie Book*, a manual for leaders, was released as a step toward establishing a standardized Brownie program, and in the same year an organizational meeting called the

First American Brownie Pow-Wow was held to bring together all those interested in formalizing the Brownies.

A year later, a National Brownie Committee was created to sort out the purpose and regulating principles of the Girl Scout Brownies, including the age level, uniform, badges, and ranks. In 1926, *The Brown Book for Brown Owls* was published as the first official leader's guide for Brownies. By 1927, Girl Scout National Headquarters stocked a brown

BELOW
A Girl Scout salutes the American flag at the first Girl Scout Camp as Juliette Low looks on, New York, 1920.

OPPOSITE ABOVE
Juliette Low and pilot Lawrence Driggs prepare to fly over Girl Scout National Headquarters in New York on November 4, 1920.

OPPOSITE BELOW
Juliette Low's funeral, Savannah, Georgia, 1927

uniform for the Brownies: a brown pullover dress with pockets and a Peter Pan collar, to be worn with brown socks and shoes, and a hat. The National Brownie Committee also identified age-appropriate activities and ceremonies for the Brownies. After completing the Brownie program, girls would "fly up" to Girl Scouts, earning their Brownie wings, which would be worn on their Girl Scout uniforms.

Even as Girl Scouts sought to expand its ranks on domestic soil, it looked to extend its reach more globally—specifically, to American girls living overseas. TOFS, United States Girl Scout Troops on Foreign Soil, was founded in 1925, giving thousands of American girls living around the world a chance to enjoy active Girl Scout troops, just like their friends in the United States. Through TOFS, troops took hold in such far-flung locations as China, Mexico, Saudi Arabia, and Singapore. The first overseas troop was organized in Shanghai, China.

Also reflecting a commitment to global awareness, Thinking Day was introduced in 1926 as a special time for troops to focus on another country's way of life. Celebrated on February 22, the birthday of both Sir Robert Baden-Powell and his wife, Olave, the day was established with the idea of making the world a smaller, friendlier, and more tolerant place by encouraging Girl Scouts and Girl Guides worldwide to "circle the globe" with thoughts of international friendship and world peace.

A third global initiative, WAGGGS, the World Association of Girl Guides and Girl Scouts, replaced

the International Council in 1928 as the primary international organizing force of Girl Scouts and Girl Guides. Today, in an age of internationalism in which some form of Girl Scouting is accessible to girls in every pocket of the world, WAGGGS can lay claim to more than 10 million members in 150 countries.

Unfortunately, not all of the changes that occurred in Girl Scouts in the 1920s were happy ones. On January 17, 1927, Juliette Low died, leaving behind a legacy that has had an impact on the lives of millions of girls. Until the very end, while bravely battling breast cancer, she remained a Girl Scout through and through. After retiring as Girl Scout President in 1920, she embraced her new role as the Founder, turning all her attention to the worldwide movement. She attended the first three international Girl Scout conferences, and in 1926 she led the fourth, at home in the United States, at Camp Edith Macy in New York, warmly welcoming participants from across the globe. Even as she endured great pain, her

First Ladies

All three First Ladies of the 1920s—Florence Harding, Grace Coolidge, and Lou Henry Hoover—accepted the now established role of National Honorary President.

SIDEBAR BELOW
First Lady Grace Coolidge, Honorary President, Girl Scouts of the USA, with Juliette Low (far right), 1926

SIDEBAR BOTTOM
Lou Henry Hoover, Honorary President, Girl Scouts of the USA

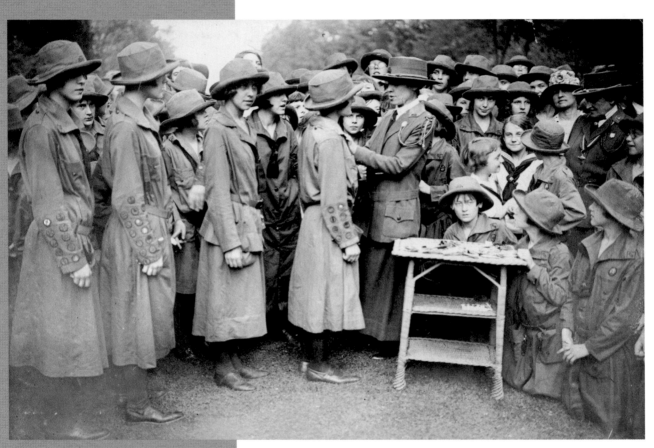

grace and perseverance modeled qualities for every Girl Scout.

The day before she died, Juliette Low received a telegram from the National Board of the Girl Scouts that read: "You are not only the first Girl Scout, but the best Girl Scout of them all." She was so touched that she asked that the telegram be placed in the pocket of her uniform, which she planned to be buried in.

Juliette Low left behind 168,000 Girl Scouts in an enduring movement that was well positioned to move forward. To this day, Girl Scouts everywhere celebrate her birthday on October 31. In addition, on Thinking Day, February 22, they honor her memory with contributions to the Juliette Low World Friendship Fund, which finances international projects and remains "dedicated forever to good will and cooperation among nations of the world."

The Girl Scouts closed the 1920s by making an important contribution to the fields of American art and history—the 1929 Loan Exhibition of Eighteenth and Early Nineteenth Century Furniture and Glass.

S'mores

If you have ever been present at a campfire, you have sampled a s'more—the word's origin is, quite clearly, "some more." In 1927, a publication titled *Tramping and Trailing with the Girl Scouts* published what appears to be the first-ever recorded recipe for s'mores, a campfire-toasted marshmallow and a piece of chocolate sandwiched between two graham crackers. All Girl Scout publications featuring s'more recipes referred to the sticky treat as a "some more" until 1971—the year the now ubiquitous contraction came into being.

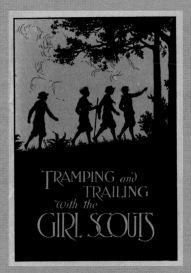

"Some More"

8 sticks

16 graham crackers
8 bars plain chocolate (Hershey's or any of the good plain brands broken in two)
16 marshmallows

Toast two marshmallows over the coals to a crisp gooey state and then put them inside a graham cracker and chocolate bar sandwich. The heat of the marshmallow between the halves of chocolate bar will melt the chocolate a bit. Though it tastes like "some more" one is really enough.

Birdsall Otis Edey

Writer and prominent Girl Scout leader Birdsall Otis Edey served as the first editor of *The Field News*, a magazine exclusively for Girl Scout leaders. A talented poet with several published collections to her name, she is also famous for penning a moving tribute to Juliette Low after her death. She led a rally of Girl Scouts in New York's Central Park in 1920, and from 1930 to 1935 she served as National President.

Birdsall Otis Edey and Girl Scouts in Central Park, New York City, 1920

Displayed in the American Art Galleries in New York City from September 25 to October 9 of that year, this collection of early American artifacts—furniture, portraits, glass, and porcelain—was assembled by Girl Scout adults and exhibited for the benefit of the National Council of Girl Scouts, Inc. Highly regarded as having "tremendous educational value to the country," published catalogs of photographs of the exhibit have become an important antique reference. Fifty years later, in 1980, another installation of American decorative arts, titled "In Praise of America," was exhibited at the National Gallery of Art in Washington, D.C., in commemoration of the 1929 Loan Exhibition.

On October 29, 1929, the carefree decade that had roared its way into and across America ended with a resounding crash. This day, now known as Black Tuesday, saw the Wall Street stock market experience a dizzying drop, and immediately faith in the national leadership dropped to an all-time low. The country was to become a very different place than it had been during the hopeful boom years at the beginning of the decade.

But the success the Girl Scouts enjoyed in the 1920s—by the close of the decade, it celebrated a membership surpassing 200,000—would pave the way for further growth and opportunity in the 1930s, despite the challenges facing the country. Indeed, Girl Scouts would step up to help the nation face those challenges head-on as it expanded its commitment to leadership, service, and the greater good.

Bertha Chapman Cady

In 1924, outdoor activities for Girl Scouts were greatly expanded, thanks to the efforts of Bertha Chapman Cady, who wrote a series of new nature projects. She developed special "nature notebooks" and wrote a series of articles that appeared each month in *The American Girl,* corresponding to five new nature badges that were introduced in 1925.

1930s

A Beacon in a Troubled World

Girl Scout Equipment·

1 · 9 · 3 · 5

The 1930s were a tumultuous decade for the country, yet an important period in Girl Scout history, reflected by a number of changes to the organization and still more growth. After the stock market crash of 1929 threw the country into a severe economic crisis, the 1930s were spent largely in recovery from the ensuing Great Depression, as Americans struggled to get back on their feet and made sacrifices to keep their families together. President Franklin Delano Roosevelt's New Deal, initiated in 1933, was intended to get Americans from all walks of life back to work, thus reinvigorating the economy. Another alarming concern was the rise of totalitarianism around the world. By the end of the decade, Adolf Hitler, Benito Mussolini, Emperor Hirohito, and Joseph Stalin had risen to power, and the seeds of World War II were sown when Japan invaded China in 1937 and Germany invaded Poland near the end of 1939.

The Great Depression permeated every corner of American life. Yet despite the extreme difficulties many parents had trying to feed and care for their families, Girl Scouting grew steadily through the 1930s—in fact, its ranks more than doubled during the course of the decade. Many children worked to provide additional income for their families, but the Girl Scout troops that persevered through the Depression grew stronger and more unified. They gained an invigorated sense of purpose and social conscience. Girl Scouts offered girls a positive focus and a consistent community—a beacon in an anxious and challenging time.

BELOW
Girl Scouts take to the radio to communicate to the world about Girl Scouting, 1934.

BOTTOM
The American Girl published a notice of Girl Scout–themed radio programs, including the organization's birthday celebrations.

But not all of the changes in the 1930s were difficult ones. The country saw exciting, positive transformations, too, with new technologies and increased growth of existing ones, like radio. In addition to providing families with news and favorite programs to gather 'round, radio allowed Girl Scouts to provide information to girls who lived in remote areas and became a useful public relations tool. Girl Scouts employed the medium to grow membership and sign up a new generation of Girl Scouts, and their broadcasts let the whole country know about their achievements. National Girl Scout leaders such as First Lady Lou Henry Hoover and Anne Hyde Choate, Juliette Low's goddaughter, made speeches over NBC radio that were heard by people in every pocket of the nation.

In 1931, Lou Henry Hoover—Honorary President of Girl Scouts—harnessed the airwaves to mobilize Girl Scouts, encouraging them to help families facing the consequences of unemployment. In response, Girl Scout troops raised money; held drives for food and clothing; and volunteered in schools, hospitals, churches, soup kitchens, and community centers— wherever they saw a need. As a result of this public call—and Girl Scouts' quick and sincere actions in response—Girl Scouts established a widespread reputation among grateful Americans as a service-oriented organization. Girl Scouts could be counted on to reach out to others.

In fact, "reaching out" became a theme of sorts for Girl Scouts in the 1930s, and while Americans in

The GIRL SCOUTS Present—
— their REPORT for 1934:

Girl Scout Radio Fans!

You'll want to listen in on these programs. Eastern Standard Time. Be sure to check time in your local newspaper.

March 13—MONDAY, P. M.
1:15-1:30 *Let's Talk it Over.*— Alma Kitchell, WEAF the N.B.C. concert singer and mis-
(Red) tress of ceremonies will interview Crestwood, N. Y., Girl Scouts who will also sing four songs accompanied by a Girl Scout orchestra.

March 15—WEDNESDAY, P. M.
4:15-4:45 *Girl Scouts 1939 Birthday Celebra-* WABC *tion Party*—presented by Columbia Broadcasting System and Girl Scout National Headquarters, with Mrs. Herbert Hoover, Mrs. Frederick H. Brooke, Girl Scouts, Jessica Drag-onette, Morton Downey, Alice Frost, and Nila Mack participating.

March 16—THURSDAY, P. M.
9:00-10:00 *Good News of 1939*— Fanny Brice WEAF and her father in a "Baby Snooks" (Red) black-out about Girl Scouting.

A full-length portrait of Lou Henry Hoover, circa 1930s

First Lady

Lou Henry Hoover was a strong, independent outdoorswoman; a Stanford graduate; a personal friend of Juliette Low's; and a lifelong participant in Girl Scouts, in one role or another. She began her relationship with Girl Scouts as the National Commissioner and spearheaded a movement to teach Girl Scouts to be actively involved in disaster response, including teaching them to grow and tend to war gardens. Like Juliette Low, she believed that all women, from homemakers to career women, should have a civic conscience and active involvement in the world around them. Lou Henry Hoover served as Girl Scouts' Vice President, as National President twice (from 1922 to 1925, and from 1935 to 1937), and as Honorary President from 1929 to 1933. She founded troops in Washington, D.C., and Palo Alto, California. Her Washington, D.C., troop was racially integrated in the 1920s, which was unusual for the time. Lou Henry Hoover was responsible for funding and creating a Little House in Palo Alto, which was used by Girl Scout leaders and as a headquarters for local members.

OPPOSITE
The New York Public Library branches in Harlem host troops
organized by Beatrice "Buddy" Price Russell, circa 1930s.

BELOW
American Indian Girl Scouts from 30 tribes attend the first American
Indian Girl Scout camp and conference in Anadarko, Oklahoma, 1933.

BOTTOM
Girl Scouts visit the 1939 New York World's Fair.

need were offered Girl Scouts' outstretched hands of help, diverse populations of American girls were offered hands of welcome. In the early part of the decade, American Indian Girl Scouts, in particular, received much attention and celebration. In 1932, *Leader* magazine devoted its entire May issue to American Indian Girl Scouts, which numbered 725 members in 35 troops nationwide (by 1935, the number of members had jumped to 1,200), and the first American Indian Girl Scout camp and conference was held in Anadarko, Oklahoma, in 1933, with 65 American Indian Girl Scouts from 30 tribes in attendance.

Girl Scouts turned its attention to newer American girls, as well. The popular promotional booklet "Who Are the Girl Scouts?," originally published in 1927, was translated into Italian, Polish, and Yiddish in 1934 to include and invite American girls from immigrant populations, and 1935 saw the integration of Chinese and Japanese girls into a Girl Scout troop in Seattle, Washington. In Hawaii, Filipino girls from sugar and pineapple plantations were attracted to the movement. African American Girl Scout troops—as well as integrated troops—had assembled steadily throughout the 1920s in cities such as New York, Boston, Washington, D.C., and Nashville. In the 1930s, new troops were founded by Lena B. Watson in Virginia, by Josephine Groves Holloway in Tennessee, and at the famed Penn Boarding School on St. Helena Island, South Carolina.

The 1938 My Community badge required

LEFT
A large-print-format handbook for girls with visual impairments, 1934

OPPOSITE ABOVE
An adult Girl Scout leader supervises a demonstration of lifesaving techniques at a public pool.

OPPOSITE BELOW
Girl Scouts practice archery at a camp in Brooklyn, New York, 1930.

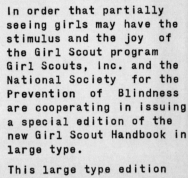

THE GIRL SCOUT HANDBOOK FOR PARTIALLY SEEING GIRLS

OCT 27 1934 RECEIVED IN FILE

In order that partially seeing girls may have the stimulus and the joy of the Girl Scout program Girl Scouts, Inc. and the National Society for the Prevention of Blindness are cooperating in issuing a special edition of the new Girl Scout Handbook in large type.

This large type edition contains the Tenderfoot and Second Class requirements and the supplementary material essential to understanding and completion of these requirements. It reproduces many of the delightful illustrations of the regular edition. It may be obtained from National Equipment Service, Girl Scouts, Inc., 570 Lexington Avenue, New York, N. Y. Price 50 cents.

that girls "find out how many racial groups and nationalities are represented in your community" and tell the story of their coming and what they did for the community. In a time when some countries were ruled by totalitarian regimes, Girl Scouts embodied a more inclusive view of the world, and one had only to look at the faces of its members to see it.

From the start, Girl Scouts had also opened its arms to girls with physical disabilities, but this decade saw the development of new ways for them to participate more fully. In 1931, increased attention was focused on Girl Scouts who were "physically handicapped," and as a result, the number of troops formed specifically for girls with disabilities increased 70 percent. National scholarships were created for leaders of troops that included girls with disabilities, including a Helen Keller scholarship for working with girls who were blind and a Fred Edey Scholarship for the leader of a "crippled" troop. Visually impaired girls were given fresh access to the *Girl Scout Handbook* when braille and large-type editions were produced in 1935, in cooperation with the American Red Cross and the National Society for the Prevention of Blindness. Also in 1935, leaders of Girl Scouts with disabilities assembled for a conference in New York City, and the following year, the first international conference of leaders for Girl Scouts and Girl Guides with disabilities was held in London.

Exciting new opportunities were created for girls of all abilities at the same time. By 1933, the number of Girl Scout camps in the United States rose

Mariner Girl Scout Dagmar Wright, Golden Eaglet, from Troop 42 in Rockville Center, New York, poses in her uniform, circa 1930s.

A Mariner troop takes to the open ocean for a sail with Golden Eaglet Kathleen Kelly at the helm, 1936.

Girl Scout Intermediate proficiency badges, 1938–1953: Outdoor Cook, World Knowledge

to 695, the greatest number in Girl Scout history. A new handbook was published that same year, with a greater focus on Girl Scouts' interests such as arts and crafts, along with a new guide for badge requirements and special awards. For Girl Scouts interested in the sea, sea lore, and navigation, the Mariner Girl Scouts was launched in 1934 with sailor-style uniforms, nautical-themed ranks (such as Jack Tar, Seaman, and Old Salt), and corresponding insignia.

On a more practical level, the ranks of Girl Scouts in general were reviewed and reassigned, and in 1938 the program was divided into three age levels—Brownies (ages 7 to 9), Intermediates (ages 10 to 13), and Seniors (ages 14 to 17), with the first Senior Girl Scout uniform made available. The new levels enhanced service and provided appropriate activities for girls of a wide range of ages. In addition, program activities were recategorized into 10 broad fields of interest, including community life, health and safety, and international friendship. On a further housekeeping note, Girl Scouts adjusted the wording surrounding badges, replacing the term *merit badge* with *proficiency badge*, emphasizing the skills and accomplishment girls acquired when earning badges. Later, in 1939, the highest award in Girl Scouts, the Golden Eaglet, was retired and replaced instead with First Class. Since its inception in 1918, the Golden Eaglet had been awarded to 10,733 Girl Scouts.

The 1930s also brought many causes for celebration in the form of landmark anniversaries, and Girl Scouts celebrated heartily with special events. In

BELOW
Girl Scout Intermediates enjoy the latest issue of *The American Girl*,
circa 1930s.

BOTTOM
Girl Scout Brownies and Intermediates participate in community
activities, circa 1937.

RIGHT
The March 1937 *American Girl* cover by Lawrence Wilbur is used on
the official Jubilee poster.

1932, March 12 was designated as Girl Scouts' official
birthday, and a grand production was arranged the
following year for the movement's 21st birthday: *The
Girl Scouts' Coming of Age Party*. Presented at New
York's Radio City Music Hall, this dramatic pageant
counted 16,000 people in attendance. The performance
was repeated in the greater New York area and then in
Chicago, featuring local girls in the cast.

The year 1937 signified Girl Scouts' 25th
anniversary, and throughout the year special events

Silver Jubilee

Twenty-five years after its founding, Girl Scouting celebrated its Silver Jubilee year. The inaugural event for the year was a nationwide radio broadcast over the blue network of the National Broadcasting Company.

The yearlong festivities included a National Jubilee Dinner and banquets in Girl Scout councils across the country. These events helped the 400,000 members of the Girl Scout organization and its many thousands of alumnae recall their Girl Scout days and tell the public more about Girl Scouting.

Girls and adults were encouraged to participate in a series of civic programs in their communities across the country. These projects included safety campaigns, health campaigns, cleanup weeks, and other civic programs of interest to the community and the Girl Scouts.

The biggest "birthday party" of all was held at the first national encampment for Girl Scouts in the United States. Girls came from every state in the union and were joined by representatives from the 31 other countries in the World Association of Girl Guides and Girl Scouts.

1930s *A Beacon in a Troubled World*

70

1912 · GIRL SCOUT SILVER JUBILEE · 1937

CAMP ANDRÉE

NATIONAL GIRL SCOUT CAMP · BRIARCLIFF MANOR · NEW YORK

SIDEBAR TOP
A scrapbook assembled by Golden Eaglet Jerrene Lucas contains autographs, photographs, and souvenirs of the Silver Jubilee at Camp Andrée.

SIDEBAR BOTTOM
A number of events were held in Savannah as part of the Jubilee.

The events of the Silver Jubilee year culminated at the 1937 Girl Scout convention held in Savannah, Georgia—a fitting place, since Girl Scouting began there 25 years earlier.

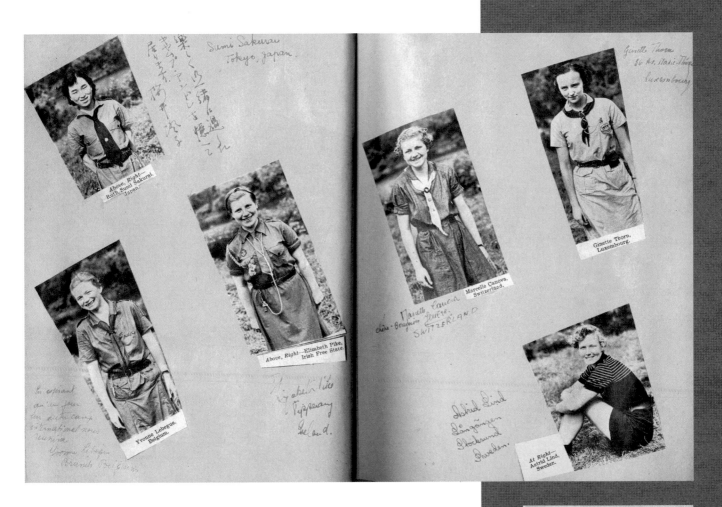

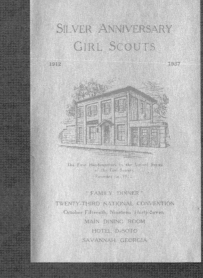

Delegates to the Second Girl Scout Western Hemisphere Encampment guide Eleanor Roosevelt on a visit to Camp Bonnie Brae, Springfield, Massachusetts, 1941.

First Lady

Eleanor Roosevelt served as the Honorary President of Girl Scouts, and a number of her famous radio addresses were given to or featured a reference to Girl Scouts. In 1934, for example, Roosevelt spoke to a large group of Girl Scouts in Boston on the subject of the "quality of a Scout." She noted that Girl Scouts were given an opportunity to get to know a wide variety of people, offering a glimpse into the worlds of ethnic diversity and economic difficulties. She also noted the importance of getting to know young people from other countries with the understanding that international friendship and goodwill was key to preventing future wars.

But it was in the close of her remarks that she made a comment that embodies the circumstances and spirit in which Juliette Low gave birth to the Girl Scout movement. Framed in a discussion of the importance of learning domestic arts and maintaining a home, Eleanor Roosevelt acknowledged that whether or not a woman has children of her own, she can have a lasting impact on young people. Juliette Low certainly did, and millions of girls and women today can thank her for "mothering" them through the Girl Scout experience.

1930s *A Beacon in a Troubled World*

72

were held to commemorate this Silver Jubilee. The festivities were kicked off with a nationwide NBC broadcast on March 12 by National President Lou Henry Hoover, and on April 9, a National Silver Jubilee Dinner was held at the Hotel Biltmore in New York, with speakers including National Honorary President First Lady Eleanor Roosevelt.

Local Girl Scout councils nationwide planned a number of events to celebrate this milestone. In true Girl Scout fashion, the events often revolved around community service—safety and health campaigns, community cleanups, child-care services at local fairs, and so on. And in August, a Silver Jubilee Camp was held at Camp Andrée, the first encampment of both American Girl Scouts and international Girl Guides held on American soil. The camp's opening ceremony was attended by 99 Girl Scouts and 26 Girl Guides from other countries, and Eleanor Roosevelt again delivered a message on world peace.

The close of the decade saw more opportunities for Girl Scouts to increase their visibility to the American people. In 1939, Girl Scout Day was celebrated at the World's Fairs in San Francisco and New York, where Girl Scouts held demonstrations of program activities and performed in pageants. A replica of Our Chalet, the WAGGGS world center in Adelboden, Switzerland, was dedicated at the New York fair.

No discussion of the 1930s would be complete without a look at the transformations in Girl Scout cookie sales. In the midst of the dark and troubling Depression, Girl Scout cookies offered a bit of sweetness and light on a broader scale than ever before as Girl Scouts turned to commercial bakeries for their production. In November 1933, the Girl Scouts of Greater Philadelphia Council sold boxes of cookies—44 cookies to a box—for 23 cents through the city's gas and electric company. After an impressive sale of 100,000 boxes in the space of a month, the council enlisted a commercial bakery for production the following year. Through the years, Girl Scout cookies have been manufactured by many different bakeries (there were as many as 30 licensed companies in the 1950s).

Girl Scout cookies became an integral part of the movement, and for a number of reasons. The selling process provided (and still does provide) important life and career skills to girls, among them planning, marketing, network-building, and sales. Selling cookies requires confidence, a self-starting mentality, perseverance, determination, and independence, not to mention an entrepreneurial spirit, math and people skills, and the ability to work together for a common cause. Through the cookie sales in the 1930s, Girl Scouts raised money to keep troops up and running, to start new troops, to support camps, and to bolster the work of their local councils. And, of course, the tasty little symbols of goodwill put smiles on the lips of anxious Americans, if just for a moment.

As the 1930s came to a close, Europe and Asia were on the verge of entering World War II, and people around the globe were about to undergo one

Girl Scout Cookies at a Glance

1910s–1920s As early as 1917, Girl Scouts baked cookies for sale to earn money. In 1922, Florence Neil of Chicago published a recipe for them in the July issue of *The American Girl* (see page 49 for recipe).

1930s Girl Scouts of the Greater Philadelphia Council enlisted a local bakery to produce cookies for sale, making it the first council to sell commercially baked cookies. By 1936, the national Girl Scouts organization began the process of licensing the first commercial baker.

1940s After a break from cookie production because of rationing during World War II, cookie sales resumed, and by 1948, 29 bakers nationwide were licensed to produce Girl Scout cookies.

1950s Three types of Girl Scout cookies were offered: Sandwich, Shortbread, and Chocolate Mints (now Thin Mints). Some local bakers also offered an optional flavor.

1960s The baby boomers entered Girl Scouts, and cookie sales skyrocketed. The number of licensed bakeries was honed to 14. Top sellers included Chocolate Mint, Shortbread, and Peanut Butter Sandwich.

SIDEBAR BELOW
Girl Scout cookie box, 1930s

SIDEBAR BOTTOM
Capital Airlines purchases enough cookies to serve in flight throughout its entire national network of 75 cities, circa 1955.

Babe Ruth poses with Girl Scout Alma Swahlin to kick off Girl Scout cookie sales, 1924.

1970s With only four licensed bakeries—allowing for maximum uniformity of quality—Girl Scouts also established consistent packaging. Boxes with the same design depicted scenes of Girl Scouts in action, usually in the outdoors.

1980s The maximum number of cookie varieties was limited to seven—the mandatory Thin Mint, Sandwich, and Shortbread cookies, plus four optional varieties.

1990s Just two commercial bakeries—Little Brownie Bakers of Louisville, Kentucky, and ABC Bakers of Richmond, Virginia—produced eight varieties of cookies. Age-appropriate awards were established for cookie sales, including an annual Girl Scout Cookie Activity Pin.

2000s–present Cookie packaging represents girls having fun and growing strong. Of the eight varieties available today, all are kosher and contain no trans fats.

In 2010 "The Five Skills for Girls" were introduced as the focus of the Girl Scout Cookie Program, based on the Girl Scout Experience. These skills include Goal Setting, Decision Making, Money Management, People Skills, and Business Ethics. In fall 2011, new Cookie Badges at each grade level were introduced, along with Daisy Girl Scout Leaves focusing on the Cookie Program. Each corresponded to a Financial Literacy Award at the same grade level.

Dr. Lillian Gilbreth

Dr. Lillian Gilbreth, born in 1878, was a time and motion study expert, engineer, industrial psychologist, and presidential advisor in addition to a loving, involved mother of 12. Her family was immortalized in the books *Cheaper by the Dozen* (1948) and *Belles on Their Toes* (1950), written by her children Ernestine and Frank Jr.; both books have been made into popular movies over the years. Dr. Gilbreth was a supporter of Girl Scouts and served as an active member of the Board of Directors.

of the most devastating periods in recorded human history. Girl Scouts of the USA grew during the 1930s by fine-tuning its structure, helping fellow Americans find food and shelter, and continuing to prepare girls for a meaningful future, regardless of their ethnicity or abilities. The organization had improved, and it emerged from a difficult decade stronger than ever, with its original mission intact and with an ever-increasing number of members.

The first mounted Girl Scout troop in the United States rides in Oakland, California, 1931.

BELOW
Equipment catalogs are the official place to shop for all things Girl Scouts in the 1930s.

OPPOSITE
Almost all the handbooks and uniform catalogs have diagrams illustrating the proper way to wear one's uniform.

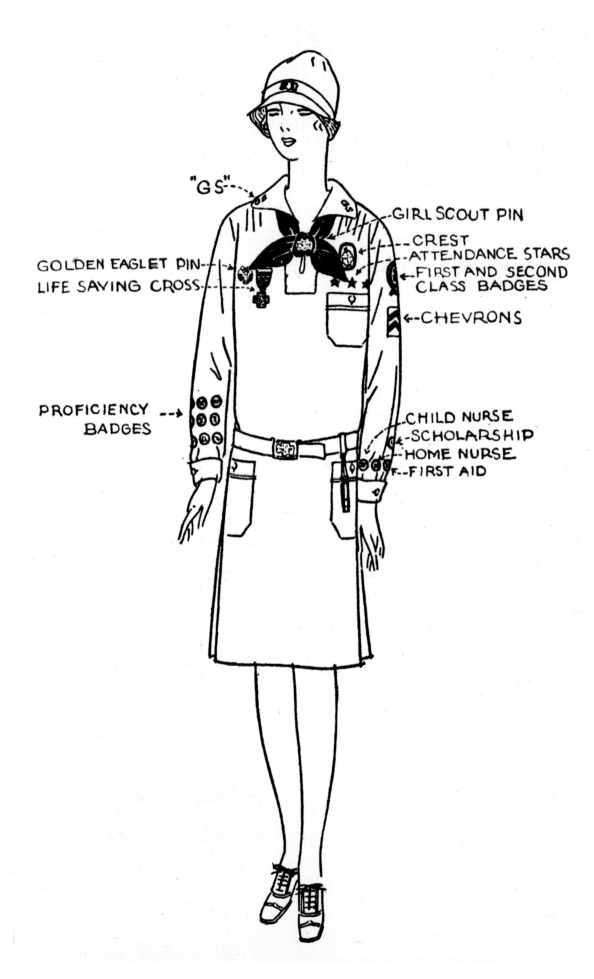

"GS"

GIRL SCOUT PIN

CREST
ATTENDANCE STARS
FIRST AND SECOND
CLASS BADGES

GOLDEN EAGLET PIN
LIFE SAVING CROSS

←CHEVRONS

PROFICIENCY
BADGES

CHILD NURSE
SCHOLARSHIP
HOME NURSE
FIRST AID

The Girl Guide and Girl Scout Chalet

One of the draws at the 1939 New York World's Fair was a carefully constructed replica of the Girl Guide and Girl Scout world center, Our Chalet, located in Adelboden, Switzerland. A store set up inside the chalet sold Girl Scout uniforms, accessories, equipment, and shoes. A patch was designed especially for the fair, in the tradition of patches that commemorated special occasions and events.

SIDEBAR LEFT
A postcard showing Our Chalet, 1939

SIDEBAR RIGHT
Girl Scout adults gather at the replica of Our Chalet at the 1939 New York World's Fair.

SIDEBAR BOTTOM
Girl Scouts perform at the 1939 New York World's Fair.

GIRL SCOUT CHALET—CHILDREN'S WORLD—N. Y. WORLD'S FAIR

Girl Scout Brownies roast marshmallows at a campfire in Pine Ridge,
New Jersey, 1936.

1940s

World at War

GIRL
SCOUT
HAND
BOOK

Two Washington, D.C., Girl Scouts sort through the collection of newspaper clippings sent to the Treasury's War Finance Division, circa 1942.

In the 1940s, the defining event for the nation—and in many ways, for Girl Scouts of the USA—was World War II. From the attack on Pearl Harbor on December 7, 1941, to the German and Japanese surrenders in 1945, the war evoked fear and brought hardship to U.S. citizens, but also provided a great opportunity for the country to come together and stand strong. For women in particular, opportunities opened up in abundance: More than 350,000 adventurous women entered all branches of the U.S. armed forces, civilian women across the country rolled up their sleeves and went to work in munitions plants, and still others rallied the country in support of the war; their activities ranged from promoting the sale of war bonds to participating in the American Red Cross and other international organizations.

Girl Scouts, more than 630,000 members strong at the beginning of the decade, stepped up as well. Carrying forward its long-established traditions of patriotism and service to others, and with a strong track record of taking action in wartime established during World War I, Girl Scouts was well poised not only to serve the country during a difficult time but also to help rebuild the world afterward, in ways big and small.

Before the United States entered the war, Girl Scouts gathered around the Christmas tree in New York's Rockefeller Center at a ceremony in 1940 to present the Girl Guides of England with gifts in support of their own war effort: an ambulance, two mobile kitchens, air raid shelter equipment, and 330 pounds of knitting wool. Princess Mary, President of the British Girl Guides, listened to the presentation from England and thanked the Girl Scouts via shortwave broadcast.

Early in 1941, in a ceremony in Washington, D.C., Girl Scouts pledged to be of service to the national defense effort in any way they could, and it wasn't long before that service was needed. When Pearl Harbor was bombed in December, the United States dove into World War II. Immediately following the announcement of the bombing, Girl Scout National Headquarters telegraphed all councils, urging them to "stick to their jobs" and reminding them of their commitment with one strong sentence: "Girl Scouting is Defense."

Throughout the war years, Girl Scouts proved themselves over and over with their dedication to service. The organization began by launching a Senior Service Scout program, a civilian defense program for Girl Scouts ages 15 to 18. Prepared in cooperation with the American Red Cross and approved by the Office of Civilian Defense, this program trained participating Girl Scouts in wartime duties ranging from messenger service, fire prevention, and first aid to signaling, survival skills, and cooking for crowds.

Volunteers for Victory, a pamphlet explaining ways Girl Scouts could become involved in war efforts in their communities, was published in 1941. Another publication, called *Senior Girl Scouting in Wartime*, was created in 1943 to encourage older girls to find

BELOW
A poster highlights one of the most important ways Girl Scouts contributed to the war effort.

BOTTOM
President Roosevelt is presented with the check for Girl Scout service hours, March 12, 1944.

OPPOSITE ABOVE
Girl Scouts participate in the National Defense effort by collecting scrap metal.

OPPOSITE BELOW
Girl Scouts in front of a Girl Scout council office load a wagon with canned goods in support of the war effort.

ways to help in hospitals, schools, and emergency situations. In addition, Girl Scouts distributed pamphlets and materials with many ideas for service projects and information on responding to air raids. Girl Scout efforts were even showcased in a 1942 motion picture also titled *Volunteers for Victory*.

As a result of these programs and pamphlets and guidance from their local troop leaders, Girl Scouts took action. Throughout the war, Girl Scouts operated bicycle courier services, invested hundreds of thousands of hours in the Farm Aide Project, and grew Victory Gardens. They collected rubber for tires, nylon and rags for parachutes, and scrap metal by the ton. They picked 7,930 pounds of milkweed pods, the fiber from which was used to fill life jackets and aviator suits. They collected necessities to be shipped to Europe, and they participated in "starvation lunches" as part of a "Share the Food" plan to raise awareness and money to fight famine overseas (on the menu was one spoonful of rice, one sardine, and one banana).

When the war—and subsequent shortages of butter, sugar, and flour—disrupted Girl Scout cookie sales, the Girl Scouts instead created and sold calendars picturing Girl Scouts engaged in wartime service activities (in fact, Girl Scout calendars are still sold to this day). On March 12, 1944, Girl Scouts' birthday, President Franklin D. Roosevelt was presented with a "check" for Girl Scout service hours invested in the war effort since 1941—an impressive 15,430,000 hours in total.

Farm Aide

In a spirit similar to that of the Victory Gardens, which were made famous in World Wars I and II, the Farm Aide Project called for Girl Scouts to get dirt under their nails and dig in for the good of America. Through this program, Senior Girl Scouts, ages 15 to 18, pitched in on farms across the country to provide farmers help and save valuable crops. In 1942 alone, more than 2,300 Girl Scouts invested more than 48,000 hours serving on farms; in 1943, more than twice that number participated, logging a total of nearly 470,000 hours. Duties included gathering eggs, tending livestock, weeding and picking crops, and preserving food.

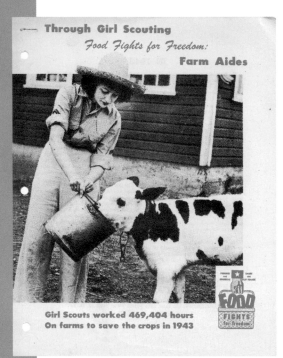

Through Girl Scouting
Food Fights for Freedom:
Farm Aides

**Girl Scouts worked 469,404 hours
On farms to save the crops in 1943**

FOOD
FIGHTS
for freedom

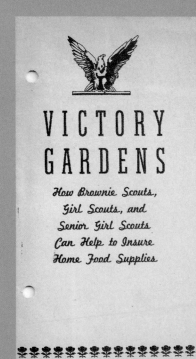

VICTORY
GARDENS

*How Brownie Scouts,
Girl Scouts, and
Senior Girl Scouts
Can Help to Insure
Home Food Supplies*

Through Girl Scouting
Food Fights for Freedom:
Victory Gardens

**15,000 Girl Scout Victory Gardens
Tended at home and in camps in 1943**

FOOD
FIGHTS
for freedom

Girl Scouts pick grapes as part of the Farm Aide Project, circa 1940s.

BELOW
Adult Girl Scout leaders listen to records, circa 1940s.

OPPOSITE
A Brownie Girl Scout holds a pet turtle, circa 1940s.

SIDEBAR OPPOSITE TOP
Volunteers for Victory was published in 1941 to support Girl Scout adult volunteer war efforts.

SIDEBAR OPPOSITE BOTTOM
Bess Truman, former First Lady and Honorary President of Girl Scouts, is presented with a set of the new Girl Scout handbooks by members of the Pioneer Trails Council, 1963.

In 1944, Girl Scouts of the USA also sent six national staff members to the United Nations Relief and Rehabilitation Administration (UNRRA) for relief work abroad. (UNRRA was replaced by the United Nations International Refugee Organization when the UN was formed in 1945.) Specifically, the six women's task was to make Girl Scouting available to displaced persons, a mission they served out at a Greek refugee camp in Palestine. In addition to fulfilling the practical needs of child welfare, repatriating refugees, and providing needed supplies, the Girl Scout representatives assisted in setting up a camping program and establishing the first National Training Camp for leaders of Greek Girl Guides.

Considering the extent of these commitments, one might draw the conclusion that war efforts totally consumed Girl Scouts and their activities during the early 1940s—but that is not true. Even while executing their many ambitious wartime service projects, Girl Scouts enjoyed more lighthearted events and accomplishments as well.

The popularity of radio and beloved crooners brought music to the ears of Americans everywhere,

Volunteers for Victory

First Lady

In 1945, First Lady Bess Truman accepted the role of National Honorary President of Girl Scouts. Considered a tomboy in her childhood, she is remembered, according to the writings of her daughter, Margaret Truman Daniel, as "a warmhearted, kind lady, with a robust sense of humor, a merry, twinkling wit, and a tremendous capacity for enjoying life."

Wing Scouts

A program for Senior Girl Scouts interested in aviation—especially as a career or as a means to serve the country—Wing Scouts was officially established in 1941. Girl Scouts had been pursuing a focus on flying since the beginning; in the first Girl Scout handbook, *How Girls Can Help Their Country*, a Flyer badge was offered, requiring Girl Scouts to "pass tests in knowledge of air currents, weather lore. Must have an aeroplane to fly 25 yards (or have a certificate for driving an aeroplane), and some knowledge of engines." And later, in 1937, a Chicago "Air Scouts" troop took off. Troop members designed their own uniforms, built model airplanes, and planned to take flying lessons as well as basic on-ground instruction.

On a national program level, this interest in aviation was worked into a general transportation project before it was formed into the Wing Scouts. Not long after the bombing of Pearl Harbor incited a keen new awareness of the importance of aviation to national defense, Girl Scouts worked with the National Aeronautic Association to develop a threefold purpose for Wing Scouts: to make girls air-minded and aware of the importance

1940s *World at War*

92

SIDEBAR BELOW
Hagarstown Packet Wing Girl Scouts admire the Piper Cub presented to them by William T. Piper, President of Piper Aircraft, 1950.

SIDEBAR BOTTOM
The *Wing Scout Manual*, published in 1945, supplements the basic Wing Scout program outlined in the handbook.

SIDEBAR OPPOSITE
A Wing Girl Scout stands next to a single-engine Piper Cub.

WING SCOUT MANUAL

and music also brought joy—and much more—to the Girl Scout movement. In 1940, the Irving Berlin Foundation arranged for the royalties from "God Bless America" to be allocated to the Girl Scout and Boy Scout organizations in the Greater New York City area, a gift in perpetuity. In 1941, *The American Girl* held a contest for "a rousing, inspirational song suitable for use by all members of the Girl Scouts," and from the influx of entries, winners were picked. First place went to "Girl Scouts Are We," by John Rivenburg, but it was the second-place song, "Girl Scouts Together," by Gladys Cornwall Goff, that endured as a longtime favorite among Girl Scouts.

The early 1940s also brought new Girl Scout honors and activities. In 1940, the Curved Bar Award was introduced, and was the highest award a Girl Scout could earn at that time. Intended for girls who had achieved First Class but who were not old enough for membership in a Senior Girl Scout troop, it honored a Girl Scout for her service as well as mature thinking and planning abilities.

In August 1940, Camp Andrée Clark played host to the first Juliette Low Western Hemisphere Encampment, which was attended by 22 Girl Scouts and Girl Guides from 13 countries and colonies in the Western Hemisphere. The following year, Camp Andrée was opened to girls in the Girl Scout Council of Greater New York for general camping use and was no longer used strictly as a testing grounds for the Senior Girl Scout program.

Also in 1941, an exciting new program was

of U.S. air supremacy, to prepare them for careers in aviation, and to prepare them for community service in aviation and allied fields. The first Wing Scouts training course, held in 1942, was sponsored by the NAA and was attended by 29 Girl Scout adults from 15 states, who brought the program home to their local troops. The program was rigorous in its requirements but extremely popular.

In 1945, a Piper Cub J-3 Trainer was presented to Girl Scouts by William T. Piper, president of the Piper Aircraft Corporation, saluting the outstanding work of Wing Scouting in the advancement of aviation training. Were the girls finally able to fly a plane? Only as passengers with a licensed instructor at the controls, and only with the consent of their parents. Nevertheless, the Piper Cub allowed them to further their ground instruction, helped them hone their skills, and no doubt inspired more than one future pilot to take the controls and fly.

World Association Pin

The World Associated Pin was introduced in 1949, and was worn by Girl Scouts and Girl Guides all over the world in an era of increased international focus and friendship. It is still available and worn proudly today to show membership in WAGGGS.

Uniforms

From the beginning of the Girl Scouts to the late 1940s, uniforms filled a fairly perfunctory role: Practical and unfussy, they offered a way for Girl Scouts to literally dress their role, create a group identity, and don a useful garment appropriate for both outdoor and indoor activities. During the early decades, the uniforms changed in color from dark blue to khaki to gray-green, with additional alterations in design.

That changed in the 1940s, when fashion began to hold more sway over the traditional practical Girl Scout uniform. In 1948, the American couturier Mainbocher designed a uniform for Intermediate, Senior, and adult Girl Scouts. The simple yet stylish green dress that resulted ensured that Girl Scouts at these levels maintained a very similar look—the cut for each level changed only to best suit the figure of each age group—and were in keeping with the fashions of the time.

SIDEBAR
The current World Association of Girl Guides and Girl Scouts (WAGGGS) badge and logo

BELOW
A Girl Scout with Wing Scout pamphlets, circa 1940s

BELOW

A poster encourages women to help the war effort by becoming Girl Scout leaders.

BOTTOM

The Liberty Ship SS *Juliette Low* is launched on May 12, 1944, in Savannah, Georgia.

THE LIBERTY SHIP "JULIETTE LOW"

See story on page 4

established—the Wing Scouts, developed for Senior Girl Scouts interested in aviation as a career or as a way of serving the country. In 1945, William T. Piper, president of the Piper Aircraft Corporation, presented the first of three Piper Cub training planes for use in this program.

Girl Scouts continued its commitment to reach out to every girl, everywhere, by forming the first Girl Scout troops in institutions for people with mental and social disabilities. The year 1946 alone saw a 40 percent increase in the number of troops for girls with physical disabilities. Girl Scouts also established troops among girls in Japanese Relocation Centers throughout the war years. In 1943, for example, troops were organized in centers in Utah, Arkansas, and California, and a 1945 report indicates that 25 Japanese American leaders from Arizona War Relocation camps attended an all-state conference in Phoenix, at which they discussed helping their Girl Scouts integrate into troops in new communities following the war.

In general, membership continued to skyrocket throughout the war years, and in 1942 a membership expansion program was announced, adding nine new major programs and a lofty goal for continuing membership growth: "A Million or More by '44." By July 1944, the campaign had succeeded with a membership count of 1,006,644. This impressive new number also represented a 300 percent increase in the number of African American Girl Scouts since just 1940.

BELOW

A canceled postcard bears a three-cent stamp designed by William K. Shrage and Ward Beeket. The stamp was issued on October 19, 1948, in Savannah, Georgia, in honor of the Girl Scouts and Juliette Low.

BOTTOM

A Girl Scout Mariner and Intermediate work together to fold a dress for the Clothes for Friendship war relief drive, circa 1940s.

On May 12, 1944, just months before this celebratory figure was announced, a great honor was bestowed upon Girl Scouts when the Liberty Ship *SS Juliette Low* was launched in Savannah, Georgia. Daisy Gordon Lawrence, Juliette Low's niece and the first member of Girl Scouts of the USA, christened the ship.

With the surrender of Germany in May 1945 and Japan in August, Americans collectively breathed a sigh of relief, celebrated the end of World War II, and began welcoming their soldiers home. The end of the war signaled an enormous shift in society, too, as women's roles began to settle back into postwar "normalcy." Still, there was much work to be done in the war's aftermath—both domestically and internationally—and women, keenly sensing this need, kept working for change. Girl Scouts, naturally, did, too.

Postwar efforts shifted to the area of relief work for countries that had been decimated during the war, leaving citizens displaced and lacking critical resources. Using funds appropriated through the Juliette Low Memorial Fund—newly renamed the Juliette Low World Friendship Fund—Girl Scouts lent a helping hand to the people of war-torn European countries in many ways. They reached out to children and youth overseas by creating brightly colored Friendship Bags that were distributed through relief agencies and contained pins, needles, thread, toothbrushes, buttons, combs, hard candy, hair ribbons, pencils or crayons, hand-knit washcloths, and a small toy. Girl Scouts also organized a Clothes for Friendship project, through which they prepared kits of children's clothing to send to European countries; at the close of this project, more than 1.5 million items of clothing had been shipped. Schoolmates Overseas, another global outreach project, enlisted Girl Scouts in assembling schoolbags containing pencils, notebooks, crayons, rulers, beanbags, and games for children in other countries.

All told, Girl Scouts contributed $50,000 from the Juliette Low World Friendship Fund to assist others in Europe and beyond. In addition to the projects mentioned above, the funds supplied powdered milk for children in Chinese orphanages, soap for people in Italy and France (replacing homemade clay soap), and fabric for uniforms in countries where Girl Guides were established. A touching request from the Girl Guides in France, published in the first annual report of the Juliette Low World Friendship Fund, included this note about the scouts' spirit overseas: "Our troops of boys and girls have struggled with all their might against the Germans. They have struggled with faith, with good humor, with tenacious will not to let themselves be defeated. . . . The Germans have taken everything except the will pledged by these young boys and girls not to bend the knee."

These relief efforts, in addition to fulfilling Girl Scouts' commitment to service, offered girls in the movement an opportunity to further their commitment to international fellowship and

understanding, a point underscored at the 11th World Conference in 1946, which gave special attention to expanding Girl Scouting and Girl Guiding throughout the world. At the 48th National Conference that same year, this commitment was underscored with an amendment to the Girl Scout Constitution that asserted: "The purpose of this organization is to help girls realize the ideals of womanhood as a preparation for their responsibilities in the home *and as active citizens in the community and in the world*." A training film (in color!) titled *The Girl Scout Leader* was also released at that conference, and copies were later purchased by the State Department to be distributed overseas as part of a program to educate other countries about life in the United States.

Girl Scouts kept their eyes on the needs of their homeland with emphasis on home safety projects through a National Home Safety campaign. This program, carried out by Girl Scouts with the Nation's Safety Council, sought to "make every home a safe home." In addition, Girl Scouts' wartime preparedness efforts, particularly in the areas of emergency and national disaster work, led to the forming of Emergency Squads at all age levels, reflecting Girl Scouts' focus on service and resourcefulness.

A final honor for Girl Scouts at the close of the decade was the issue of a three-cent commemorative stamp honoring Juliette Low. This stamp, issued by the United States Post Office, was important not only for the honor it bestowed but also because it signified Girl Scouts as an intrinsic part of the American

Juliette Low World Friendship Fund

After Juliette Low's death in 1927, a fund—the Juliette Low Memorial Fund—was established in her honor. It would be used to fund international projects. In keeping with this early intention, the fund was renamed in 1943, becoming the Juliette Low World Friendship Fund, fitting during a decade when Girls Scouts reached out to help people all over Europe who were struggling with the effects of World War II. In fact, this fund, which Girl Scouts built literally penny by penny, offered $50,000 to postwar recovery efforts in more than a dozen European countries, as well as in the Philippines, China, and Russia.

Though it was written before the war effort was in full swing, a February 1941 *Leader* article titled "Thinking Day 1941," by Arethusa F. G. Leigh-White, Director of the World Bureau of Girl Guides and Girl Scouts, well summed up the spirit of Girl Scouts and their contributions to the world during war and peace. Leigh-White reminded readers that Girl Scouts and Girl Guides everywhere are "members of a world-wide sisterhood and that, no matter to what race or creed we belong, we are united in a spirit of good will one towards the other; a spirit animated by a true

fabric. Representing girls of all types and radiating pride in its nation, the organization had become a microcosm of America itself. As a world ambassador, Girl Scouts was America's best face put forward.

BELOW
Girl Scouts and International Girl Scouts and Guides form a trefoil at the 12th WAGGGS Conference, Cooperstown, New York, August 1948.

BOTTOM
The flags are raised at the Edith Macy Conference Center in 1947.

SIDEBAR
The annual report of the Juliette Low World Friendship Fund for 1944 details how every penny of the fund is spent throughout the world.

desire for friendship." She quoted an old Irish saying—"God likes a little help"—in further reminding readers that small acts add up to great accomplishments. So it was with the Girl Scouts' many war and postwar projects, and so it was with the pennies that tallied up to offer significant aid to a hurting world through the Juliette Low World Friendship Fund.

1950s

The Boom Years

1956 GIRL SCOUT SENIOR ROUNDUP

N

W

E

S

ROUNDUP HANDYBOOK

GIRL SCOUT SENIOR ROUNDUP | **JUNE 28—JULY 11, 1956**

MILFORD, MICHIGAN

Many Americans remember the 1950s fondly, and for good reason. The nation was enjoying prosperity and peace, leisure time and cocktail hours, Ed Sullivan and Elvis Presley. Fashion evolved to showcase womanhood—or at least an idealized version of it—with the dainty waists and full, blossoming skirts that marked the "flower woman" style of Christian Dior's signature New Look. Women's roles became somewhat idealized, too—especially that of the homemaker who effortlessly ran a flawless household, as illustrated by icons of the decade such as the television character June Cleaver. Other memorable icons, including Lucille Ball, proved a woman could be whip-smart and funny, while others (think Elizabeth Taylor and Marilyn Monroe) ensnared their fans with a complicated, sultry side. Women could be athletes, like African American tennis star Althea Gibson, and, increasingly, they could be professionals.

The 1950s were boom years for Girl Scouts, too, and just as bursting with hope and opportunity. In 1950, Girl Scouts of the USA was reincorporated under a congressional charter, an honor that designated Girl Scouts as being officially sanctioned by the U.S. government. Signed by Harry Truman, the charter stated Girl Scouts' purpose as "to promote the qualities of truth, loyalty, helpfulness, friendliness, courtesy, purity, kindness, obedience, cheerfulness, thriftiness, and kindred virtues among girls, as a preparation for their responsibilities in the home and for service to the community . . . with the highest

Students practice marketing skills at the Edith Macy Training School, 1950.

BELOW
Students participate in a panel discussion at the Edith Macy Training
School, circa 1950s.

BOTTOM
Participants in the 1954 International Conference for Leaders on the
steps of Great Hall, Edith Macy Training School.

ideals of character, patriotism, conduct and
attainment." In addition, the charter gave Girl Scouts
of the USA sole ownership of all its trademarks
and emblems. In 1951, Girl Scouts received another
national honor when it was given a Freedoms
Foundation award for "outstanding contributions to
freedom" and for "significant work in building a better
understanding of the American way of life." Also in
1951, Camp Edith Macy celebrated its 25th year as
a training school for leaders and received special
recognition from the New York State Department
of Education.

A generation of postwar baby boomers began to
be born in the mid-1940s, ensuring that Girl Scouts'
membership—1.5 million strong in 1950 and positively
exploding—would continue to grow in this decade.
Girl Scouts of the era recall this as a time when it
seemed *everyone* was a Girl Scout. If a troop was
present in a girl's area—and it almost certainly was—
there was little doubt she would be in it.

A fresh focus was placed on teenage girls in
this decade with the University of Michigan's *Study
of Adolescent Girls* and the Girl Scouts' own *Girl
Scout Program Study*. The former was a thorough
examination of—and became a standard reference
for—the hopes, fears, plans and aspirations, activities,
and interests of girls ages 11 to 18. More specific to
the needs of Girl Scouts, the 1958 *Girl Scout Program
Study* evaluated the program's ability to meet the
current needs and interests of teen girls and offered
a blueprint for new programming geared especially

BELOW
Senior Girl Scouts at the All-States Camp, Pennsylvania, 1959

BOTTOM
The first Senior Girl Scout Roundup is held in Milford, Michigan, in the summer of 1956.

for older girls. In addition, in 1957 a Girl Advisory Committee to the National Program Committee was formed to ensure that girls had a voice in national program planning.

Senior Girl Scouts also enjoyed what became significant gatherings during the 1950s. In 1950, in response to older Girl Scouts' requests for a more challenging, deep-woods camping experience, the first All-States Camp for Senior Girl Scouts was held in Cody, Wyoming. The girls themselves were given the responsibility of developing a rigorous program that included cooking, sleeping out, using a compass to navigate their way, and planning camp activities. The Girl Scouts enthusiastically met these tasks, and the All-States Camp became an annual tradition for 18 years.

Yet this camp was only the first of the important gatherings planned for Senior Scouts in the 1950s. The Girl Scout Senior Roundups were another massive, memorable event, held four times between the mid-1950s and the mid-1960s. The first of these special encampments was held in 1956 in Milford, Michigan, and was intended to give Senior Girl Scouts a sense of belonging to the organization along with a chance to meet and work both with Girl Scouts from across the United States and with Girl Guides invited from other countries.

To give an idea of the scale and impact of this event, which was attended by 5,000 teenage girls, two days each had to be allowed simply for arrival and departure, respectively. Local newspapers reported long lines of cars winding down the mile-long road

BELOW
Senior Girl Scouts pose with signs of their home states at the first All-States Camp, Wyoming, 1950s.

SIDEBAR
Mamie Moore and Ellen Moore, members of Troop 288, present the first box of 1953 Girl Scout cookies to their aunt, Mrs. Dwight Eisenhower, at the White House. With them are Girl Scouts from Troop 415 of Washington, and Troop 42 of Fairfax, Virginia.

First Lady

In 1953, Mamie Doud Eisenhower became Honorary National President of the Girl Scouts. Known for her skill as a hostess, honed over many years as the wife of a military man and university professor, she gained a reputation as a "regular gal," and Americans admired her modern hairstyle, unpretentious ways, and famous fudge recipe.

to camp. To accommodate the campers, a massive tent city was set up incredibly quickly, in addition to a 2,000-car parking lot, and whole-group events had to be held in a large arena. First Lady and National Honorary President Mamie Doud Eisenhower delivered the opening greetings. Security was provided by the Michigan State Police, who set up a portable headquarters at the camp; the local post office was swamped with letters home; Western Union lines buzzed with messages to parents requesting more warm clothes. The Roundup was as memorable to the Michigan community as it was to the Girl Scouts themselves; one local account reported that "every girl you will meet is just bubbling with enthusiasm and every last one will tell you that she's making 'just piles of new friends.'"

Divided into patrols of eight girls each, the Girl Scouts and Girl Guides lived together for 12 days, doing their own cooking and outdoor housekeeping,

Roundups

The Girl Scout Senior Roundups, held four times from 1956 to 1965, offered girls a sense of connection to the greater organization, introduced them to Girl Scouts from across the nation and Girl Guides from around the world, and, as might be expected, were a tremendous amount of fun. Highlights for the participants included sharing with other Girl Scouts the particular history, characteristics, and customs of their part of the country and also celebrating the common history, songs, slogans, and practices they shared through Girl Scouts. All were unique, yet all were one.

The four Roundups were held in a different region of the United States, allowing girls to experience a new part of the country and a unique environment with each one. The sites were a state park in Milford, Michigan, in 1956; the mountainous Colorado Springs, Colorado, in 1959; the shores of Lake Champlain near Middlebury, Vermont, in 1962; and the Farragut Wildlife Management Area in Coeur d'Alene, Idaho, in 1965.

SIDEBAR FROM TOP TO BOTTOM
Roundup patches: 1956, 1959, 1962
A section from a Roundup pennant, 1965
Girl Scout Seniors pose with swap hats, 1962

SIDEBAR LEFT
Swap hats were popular at Roundups in the 1950s and 1960s. Girl Scouts would trade pins and other insignia at the events.

BELOW
Senior Girl Scouts help to set up the Senior Roundup encampment, Milford, Michigan, 1956.

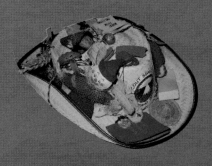

The first Girl Scout Senior Roundup required a massive organizational effort. For 12 days, 5,000 Girl Scouts lived together in a tent city, doing their own cooking and outdoor housekeeping.

and sharing Girl Scout history as well as the unique characteristics of their own part of the world. In addition to the enormous amount of fun and energy it generated, the Roundup illustrated the very vastness of the Girl Scout movement.

The second Roundup, in 1959, was held near Colorado Springs, Colorado, and was attended by 8,500 campers and 1,500 adult volunteers. Girls came from every state and territory, plus 24 other countries, shipped in by car, bus, plane, and train. The slogan of that year's event—"A Mile High, a World Wide"— neatly sums up the reach and influence Girl Scouts achieved in this decade.

Changes took place closer to home for Girl Scout troops as well. New handbooks were issued—a new *Brownie Scout Handbook* appeared in 1951, for the first time offering Brownies a book for their own use (rather than the "packets" of the past, which were developed for adult training), and the *Girl Scout Handbook* was revised throughout the decade to offer new ideas, activities, and energy for Girl Scouts at all levels. A 1956 *Senior Leader's Guide* for troop leaders was published; it included a declaration of purpose that encapsulated Juliette Low's original mission neatly: "The Girl Scout organization is dedicated to helping girls develop as happy, resourceful individuals willing to share their abilities as citizens in their homes, their communities, their country and the world."

In 1951, Girl Scouts of the USA signed with the United States Army to aid military dependent girls in Europe and North Africa. Girl Scouts continued to live out that mission the way they always had— with arms open to every girl. In 1952, Girl Scouting embraced the daughters of agricultural migrant workers for the first time, and in 1953 Troops on Foreign Soil expanded its reach to serve Girl Scouts living in Japan, Taiwan, and Korea through U.S.A. Girl Scouts–Far East. Girl Scouts with disabilities were better served with the publication of *Working with the Handicapped*, a definitive manual written by specialists for leaders working with Girl Scouts with physical, mental, and social disabilities. And *Ebony* magazine, in its March 1952 issue, offered accolades to Girl Scouts for the impact it was having on the growing civil rights movement. "Girl Scouts in the South," the comment read, "are making steady progress toward breaking down many of the region's racial taboos." In 1956, Martin Luther King Jr. called Girl Scouts a "force for desegregation."

Always progressive when it came to social issues like civil rights, Girl Scouts had from its earliest days encouraged integration in their troops. In fact, it's impossible to identify when Girl Scouts "began" integration—it's something that happened from the very beginning. At a time when water fountains for black people and white people were still separate in many parts of the country, Girl Scouts stood up for acceptance and inclusion. They'd simply never done it any other way. "Separate but equal" was the way of life for many Americans, but it was not the way Girl Scouts operated. When Juliette Low laid out her plans

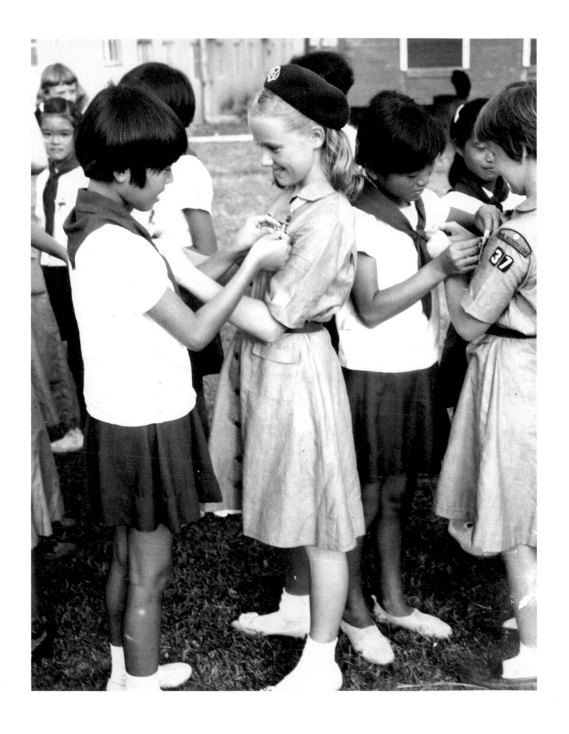

BELOW
A Girl Scout Intermediate makes her Girl Scout Promise at an investiture ceremony, 1950.

BOTTOM
The dedication ceremony for the Juliette Gordon Low Birthplace, October 1956

OPPOSITE
Two 10-year-old Girl Scouts in Montabello, California, show the proper way to cross a street, 1955.

for something for the girls of "all America," she meant *all* America, period.

And the girls of America found ways to thank her, even long after her death. In 1953, they collected and contributed "Dimes for Daisy" to purchase her childhood home in Savannah, Georgia, and fully restore and furnish it, transforming it into a National Program Center for Girl Scouts and a living memorial to Juliette Low.

With a goal of restoring the large Regency-style house to its documented appearance in 1886, the year of Juliette Low's wedding and a year when extensive changes were made to the house, the restoration project marked Girl Scouts' commitment to historic preservation at a time when the preservation movement was just getting started across the country. After three years of work, the Juliette Gordon Low Birthplace was dedicated on October 19, 1956. The Birthplace is a beloved and popular destination for Girl Scout troops, school groups, and the general touring public, as well as a valuable resource and "home" for Girl Scouts. The house is furnished with many original family pieces and a wealth of artwork by Juliette Low that illustrates the lively stories of life in the Gordon household.

Annually, thousands of Girl Scouts travel from across the country to spend an entire day at the Birthplace for a Girl Scout Heritage Visit, the culmination of years of planning, earning money, and anticipation for their troops. After exploring the life and times of the Founder through hands-on activities

and tours, Girl Scouts earn the Birthplace Pin, which symbolizes that they are now "Daughters of the House."

The decade of the 1950s closed on future-facing accomplishments. By 1957, Girl Scout membership had reached 3 million, reflecting an increase of more than 1 million in just four years. The National Headquarters in New York City moved into its own very modern building at 830 Third Avenue, one of the first skyscrapers on Third Avenue and a pioneer in architecture. Girl Scouts continued a commitment to the environment by performing more than 35,000 Outdoor Good Turns, conservation projects aimed at beautifying and cleaning up neighborhoods. Reflecting a new commitment to arts programming, Girl Scouts rolled out an educational television series, *Adventuring in the Hand Arts*, in 1958. A mobile arts unit, the Arts Caravan, toured the country in 1959 and 1960, boosting the arts education skills of 1,300 Girl Scout volunteers on its travels.

All told, the boom years of the 1950s represented much more than progress for Girl Scouts. The progress the movement enjoyed was passed on through community service and world fellowship. The sheer energy and fun generated at troop, national, and international activities couldn't help but bubble over into the community, the nation, and the world at large. The power of girls with a positive focus and a mandate to make the world a better place could see no boundaries.

Our Cabaña

The first WAGGGS world center in the Western Hemisphere—called Our Cabaña—was opened in Cuernavaca, Mexico, on July 24, 1957. Our Cabaña is the third WAGGGS world center, joining Our Chalet in Adelboden, Switzerland, and Our Ark, opened in London in May 1939 (it was renamed Olave House in 1963).

Kits for Korea

Girl Scouts all over America banded together to assemble shipments of what the organization called "Kits for Korea"—drawstring pouches filled with items needed by Korean civilians, such as soap, shampoo, and sewing supplies—as part of American Relief for Korea.

SIDEBAR LEFT
Preparing "Kits for Korea," 1951

SIDEBAR BELOW
Girl Scouts at Our Cabaña International Scout Center in Cuernavaca, Mexico, circa 1950s

SIDEBAR BOTTOM
The Central Los Angeles Council of Girl Scouts prepares "Kits for Korea," 1954.

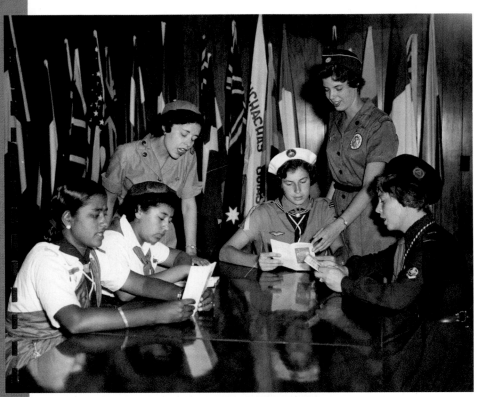

BELOW
Brownie, Intermediate, and Senior Girl Scouts walk together on the Golden Gate Bridge, San Francisco, California, circa 1950s.

SIDEBAR
The *Say It—In Another Language* pamphlet helps Girl Scouts with international communication at Roundups, 1952.

Uniforms

In 1951, updated uniforms were created to suit older Intermediate and Senior Girl Scouts, distinguishing them from their younger counterparts. Fashionable yet utterly practical, they featured a white blouse with Girl Scout insignia paired with a fuller-cut dark green skirt, in keeping with the style of the times. Adult Girl Scout uniforms featured tailored jackets and sleek pencil skirts, utterly 1950s. The famous American milliner Sally Victor topped the adult look with a pillbox beret in 1953.

Say It— In Another Language

In anticipation of the 1959 Girl Scout Roundup, the *Say It—In Another Language* pamphlet was published and distributed to Girl Scouts around the country. The pamphlet encouraged girls to learn a foreign language, such as German, Japanese, French, or Spanish.

Girl Scouts Sing!

Whether the low, mesmerizing sound of girls singing around a campfire, the rousing chant of a marching song, the patriotic classics, or the folksy rounds so many of us know by heart, music—and especially singing—has always been a rich and unifying tradition for Girl Scouts. From the very beginnings of the movement, they've known that nothing focuses and inspires a group like a much-loved song.

As early as 1917, Girl Scouts was copyrighting and publishing its own music: the words and music to "Good-Night Song," written by Ruth L. Briggs and dedicated to the first national Girl Scout Training School, and "Onward," written by Marion C. Moreland and dedicated to Wild Rose Troop #11, were both published in a pamphlet that year and sold for 15 cents.

The first "official" *Girl Scout Songbook* was compiled and published by Girl Scouts in 1925, with selections that the songbook committee deemed "appropriate for Sunday and weekday, for home and camp, rainy evening and daytime hike." It contained songs that continue to be published and sung by Girl Scouts decades later: "The Keeper," "Skye Boat Song," "All Through the Night," and "Now the Day Is Over."

The *Sing Together* songbook, compiled by Janet E. Tobitt, collected these and other beloved tunes in a publication that was revised, updated, and reorganized for decades. The book included several pages of blank scores, on which Girl Scouts were encouraged to "capture a tune in faraway places."

The *Girl Scout Songbook* and *Sing Together* were merged into a new edition of *Sing Together* in 1949, a rousing collection of action and dance songs, ceremonial songs, hiking songs, and more. Over time, some songs were omitted due to infrequent use or because they might be objectionable to certain groups. Another republication and reorganization took place in 1957, and a 1973 edition reflects the folk songs of that era.

All these songs became a sort of oral history of the Girl Scouts, telling the stories of the eras in which they appeared, yet enduring as timeless favorites. In addition to setting a tone for meetings, ceremonies, and other events, the common songs ensured that all Girl Scouts, wherever they may be in the nation or world, were literally singing the same tune. Whether they gathered at Roundups or WAGGGS events, regardless of the fact that they'd never met before and might never again, all Girl Scouts were able to raise their voices as one, in a single powerful, beautiful song.

BELOW
A page from the Fall 1958–Spring 1959 Girl Scout National Equipment
Service catalog showing a variety of Girl Scout merchandise

BOTTOM
Camping accessories are offered in the Spring 1955 Girl Scout
National Equipment Service catalog.

SIDEBAR
The Girl Scout statuette as it appears in the Fall 1958–Spring 1959 Girl
Scout National Equipment Service catalog

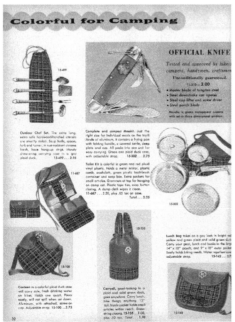

The Girl Scout Statuette

The Girl Scout statuette, sculpted by Marjorie Daingerfield, was introduced in 1954. Depicting a Girl Scout in uniform and set on a square base with a nameplate for engraving the name of the recipient, the statuette was intended as a token of appreciation for an individual or group, and would be equally appropriate as a decoration for a troop meeting room or an office.

Nat King Cole

A hot-ticket item in Robert Sylvester's column "Dream Street Beat" in the *New York Daily News* on Saturday, August 20, 1955, demonstrated the central role of Girl Scouts in 1950s American life. After a concert at the Hollywood Bowl, Nat King Cole was told that he had broken the stadium's attendance record, received a telegram informing him that six of his songs had just made the best-selling list, and learned that Universal-International was releasing a movie about him worldwide. Sylvester reported that Cole answered a phone call in his presence, listened for a while, and then announced, "Whaddya know? My daughter, Cookie, just became a Brownie!"

1960s

Honor the Past, Serve the Future

brownie
Girl Scout Handbook

JUNIOR
GIRL SCOUT HANDBOOK

cadette
Girl Scout Handbook

senior
girl scout handbook

The decade of the 1960s revealed the discomfort of a nation shifting on cultural tectonic plates, and it embodied everything from hope to tragedy to enormous progress to utter chaos. The 1960s are remembered for the establishment of the Peace Corps, the incomparable "I Have a Dream" speech, the Civil Rights Acts, and the moon landing. But they're also marked by the assassinations of President John F. Kennedy, Malcolm X, Martin Luther King Jr., and Robert Kennedy. Women took a stand for themselves and their rights when Betty Friedan founded the National Organization for Women and Gloria Steinem became the face of Women's Liberation. Rachel Carson took a stand for the environment with her penning of *Silent Spring*, and it seemed that everywhere people were standing up, speaking out, and creating tidal waves of change.

Young people were often at the forefront of this movement, with a burgeoning stake in the country's politics as young men were drafted into service in the Vietnam conflict. The decade closed on a frenzy of music, freedom, and wildness summed up perfectly at Woodstock.

Girl Scouts, in this shifting era, took a stand for what they'd always believed in: faith in their country, equal opportunity for all, tolerance, and global understanding. In a highly charged, rapidly changing time, the movement helped girls stay steady and focused on progress. True, young people could effect change by acting out, but they could also do so by establishing and living out deeply held principles.

Girl Scouts remained the beacon it was when the country was enduring the Great Depression, but for very different reasons. In the 1960s, it offered girls a sort of moral compass, an outlet for positive activity and positive change.

For Girl Scouts, the decade began on a happy note—with a birthday party. In honor of the 100th anniversary of Founder Juliette Low's birthday (October 31, 1860) and the 50th anniversary of the founding of Girl Scouts (March 12, 1912), the Birthday Years, spanning October 1960 to October 1963, were designated a movement-wide celebration. The festivities began with Founder's Day events in 1960, on Juliette Low's birthday, honoring local Girl Scout troop founders and culminating in a gala celebration at the Juliette Gordon Low Birthplace. A theme for the Birthday Years was introduced in November at the 35th National Council meeting: "Honor the Past, Serve the Future." A special Centennial Patch was worn by Girl Scouts and adult volunteers during this period.

A beautiful and highly visible "birthday gift" was bestowed on the nation in the form of flowers—yellow ones, everywhere. Girl Scouts planted them along highways; in parks and at home; and on the grounds of schools, hospitals, libraries, and places of worship, where they bloomed in spring of 1962 for Girl Scouts' 50th anniversary. The flowers in particular were a yellow floribunda rose, developed specifically for Girl Scouts, and a dwarf marigold representing Brownies. In addition, flowers of countless other varieties were

Blossoms for Birthday Years

As a tangible commemoration of the Girl Scout Birthday Years, yellow and gold flowers of all types were planted in public places, in gardens, and along highways by Girl Scouts all over the United States. Thanks to plans laid well ahead of time and to the efforts of bulb growers in Holland, seed developers, and nursery owners, the project was a blooming success.

Best of all were two flowers custom-cultivated just for the event: a Girl Scout rose (a yellow floribunda) developed by Jackson and Perkins as a tribute to Girl Scouting, and a Brownie Scout marigold, a dwarf variety that was mostly green and gold, with a touch of brown. In 1962, Girl Scout rose gardens bloomed at the Seattle World's Fair and at the Juliette Gordon Low Birthplace in Savannah.

a rose
   is a
rose
   is a
girl scout
rose

SIDEBAR
A Girl Scout Birthday Years publication, 1962

BELOW
An Intermediate Girl Scout sits in a field of daisies, circa 1960s.
(Girl Scouts celebrated the 100th birthday of their Founder, Juliette "Daisy" Gordon Low, in 1960.)

BELOW
Troops on Foreign Soil whose parents were employed by the Arabian American Oil Company in Saudi Arabia learn desert lore from guide Sa'ad iban Fahd al-Qahtani, 1960.

BOTTOM
A proclamation from the Girl Scout National Board of Directors sent by telegram to President Lyndon Johnson, Vice President Hubert Humphrey, and Judge Otto Kerner, Chairman of the National Advisory Commission on Civil Disorders, as it appeared in *Leader* magazine, October 1968. This proclamation was also sent by letter to every member of the Commission, every member of Congress, and every Girl Scout council president.

planted—daffodils, tulips, chrysanthemums, to name a few—all in yellow or gold.

Heritage Hikes were planned by councils as a celebratory activity and a way to explore historic sites in their own communities—especially exciting for Girl Scouts who were members of Troops on Foreign Soil and for whom "local sites" included the home of Shakespeare's Juliet in Verona, Italy, or the 26-mile path from Marathon to Athens in Greece. On the 50th anniversary of Girl Scouting, March 12, 1962, members of the Girl Advisory Committee to the National Program Committee presented a report at a congressional luncheon in Washington, D.C., pledging continued service to the youth of their community in honor of the Birthday Years.

It's fitting that in the midst of these celebratory years, the third Girl Scout Senior Roundup was held, this time in Button Bay, Vermont, in 1962. Located on Lake Champlain, this Roundup echoed the theme of the Birthday Years—"Honor the Past, Serve the Future"—and the participants were called to serve by President John F. Kennedy himself. Challenged by the president to prepare themselves for "service to your country and mankind," the girls held forums titled "Ideas Changing the World" and "I Shape the World," and closed the Roundup by sending President Kennedy their personal commitment to renew their pledge to the Girl Scout Promise and Laws, seek knowledge, eliminate prejudice, and promote peace, among many other earnest goals. The infectious energy and deep commitment to service espoused by

WESTERN UNION

CALL LETTERS FTC-PD   CHARGE TO GIRL SCOUTS OF THE U.S.A.   MAY 24, 1968
PRESIDENT LYNDON B. JOHNSON
THE WHITE HOUSE
WASHINGTON, D.C.

AS CITIZENS CONCERNED ABOUT SOCIAL JUSTICE AND SOCIAL UNREST, WE THE BOARD OF DIRECTORS OF GIRL SCOUTS OF THE U.S.A. VOTED THIS DAY TO SUPPORT THE MAJOR GOAL AND OBJECTIVES OF THE REPORT OF THE NATIONAL ADVISORY COMMISSION ON CIVIL DISORDERS. WE URGE ALL OUR COUNCILS TO STUDY THE FINDINGS OF THE REPORT AND TO IMPLEMENT IN EVERY WAY POSSIBLE THROUGH OUR PROGRAM THE CREATION OF "A TRUE UNION – A SINGLE SOCIETY AND A SINGLE AMERICAN IDENTITY." WE FURTHER URGE OUR COUNCILS AND OUR MEMBERSHIP TO JOIN WITH OTHER YOUTH GROUPS, OTHER COMMUNITY ORGANIZATIONS, AND OTHER INDIVIDUALS IN WORKING TOWARD THIS END.
                              MRS. HOLTON R. PRICE, JR.
                              NATIONAL PRESIDENT
                              GIRL SCOUTS OF THE U.S.A.

BELOW
The fourth and final Girl Scout Senior Roundup, held in Coeur d'Alene, Idaho, was attended by 9,000 girls and 2,000 adult leaders, July 1965.

OPPOSITE ABOVE
A Senior Girl Scout in a recording studio at the 1965 Senior Girl Scout Roundup

OPPOSITE BELOW
Girl Scout correspondents write articles for hometown newspapers at the third Girl Scout Senior Roundup in Button Bay State Park, Vermont, 1962. The theme of this Roundup is "Honor the Past, Serve the Future."

this young president found an eager audience among the Girl Scouts of the USA.

The fourth and final Roundup took place in 1965 in Coeur d'Alene, Idaho, in the Farragut Wildlife Management Area. Hosting 9,000 Girl Scouts and 2,000 adult volunteers, this Roundup was of an environmental bent, and it featured daylong conservation tours of the Kaniksu National Forest led by expert Forest Service guides, as well as the planting of 1,084 ponderosa seedlings at Farragut.

A fifth Roundup was projected for 1968, but the conflict in Vietnam interfered. Another Senior

Girl Scout program planned for 1968, Council Opportunities (later renamed Wider Opportunities), was expanded to take its place. Available to Girl Scouts from all over the country and with the goal of providing Girl Scouts with various cultural experiences, "Wider Ops" succeeded in fulfilling many of the objectives of the Roundups. In 1968, Girl Scouts also opened its National Center West in Ten Sleep, Wyoming, in the Bighorn Mountains. For 20 years, this 14,000-acre site acted as camping grounds and as a national activity center for outdoor programming and international activities, and offered Girl Scouts

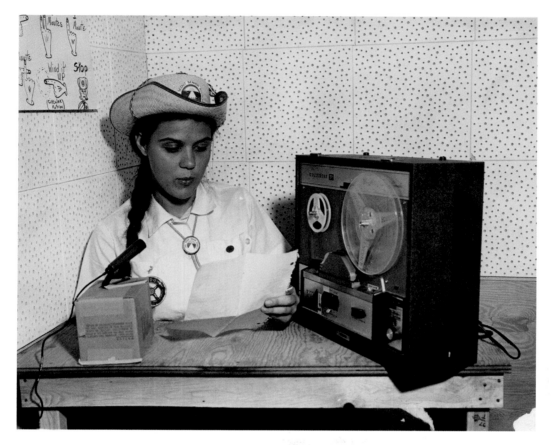

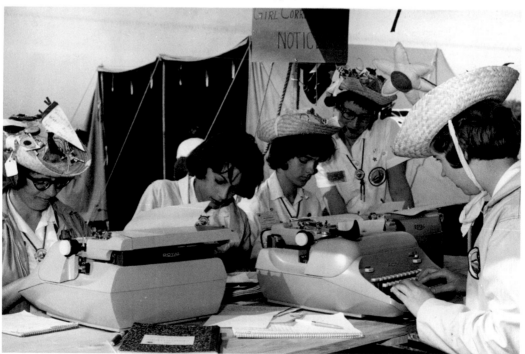

OPPOSITE ABOVE
Girl Scout Cadettes hike along a wooded trail in central New York.

OPPOSITE BELOW
Girl Scouts sit around a campfire at night singing, 1963.

yet another opportunity to experience the beauty of nature, learn to conserve natural resources, and explore the unique history and culture of a region.

Girl Scouts took up the decade's spirit of change by implementing their own changes, with the purpose of better serving the needs of Girl Scouts at every age level. In the late 1950s, study began on the current needs of adolescent girls in relation to the Girl Scout program, which led to a massive reorganization of age levels and a redesign of programs for each. A report proposing this redesign, *The Framework for Progression*, was released in 1960 and was enthusiastically received. The revised program, launched in 1963, established four distinct categories of Girl Scouts: Brownie (ages 7 to 9), Junior (ages 9 to 11), Cadette (ages 11 to 14), and Senior (ages 14 to 17). Each level received newly rewritten handbooks featuring age-appropriate programming, updated uniforms, and appropriate accessories.

Girl Scouts also expanded into mainstream book publishing when Random House published the first four titles in the *American Girl* Library series in 1963. Each one was a collection of stories or letters from the Girl Scout magazine *The American Girl*. The first three books featured horse stories, first date stories, and Pat Downing mysteries, respectively, and the fourth book consisted of teenagers' questions that had appeared in the magazine over the years.

Service continued to be a major focus of Girl Scouts, and this commitment was honored and rewarded in 1964 when Girl Scouts received Reader's

American Girl Library Series

Girl Scouts was no stranger to book publishing. The organization had published countless editions of handbooks itself and had published two collections of short stories in the 1920s; it had also been the subject of several fiction series published throughout the 1920s—some approved by the Girl Scout organization, some not. But in 1963, Girl Scouts came out with its very own series—the *American Girl* Library—published by Random House and made available to a wide market. Collections of pieces from *The American Girl* magazine, the series included:

The American Girl Book of Horse Stories
The American Girl Book of First Date Stories
The American Girl Book of Pat Downing Stories
The American Girl Book of Teen-age Questions
The American Girl Book of Mystery and Suspense
The American Girl Beauty Book
The American Girl Library Book— The Mystery of the Water Witch
The American Girl Book of Sports Stories
The American Girl Book of Dog Stories
When Girls Meet Boys

BELOW AND OPPOSITE ABOVE
Brownies and Junior Girl Scouts with actress Debbie Reynolds,
Honorary National Piper, 1966–1968

OPPOSITE BELOW
The four levels of Girl Scouts with leaders, 1960

Digest Foundation grants intended to assist Senior Girl Scout troops in undertaking community service projects. Girl Scouts' efforts toward inclusivity were further expanded when the American Printing House for the Blind published all the new handbooks for Brownie, Junior, Cadette, and Senior levels of Girl Scouts in braille, and 1964 also saw the designation of special funds to extend Girl Scout membership to girls in urban areas. Girl Scouts' membership continued to grow exponentially, with more than 1 million girls joining. The total membership that year was 3,660,814.

In 1966, a three-year membership extension plan called the Piper Project was introduced at the National Council meeting in Detroit, with the goal of retaining and further increasing Girl Scout membership, particularly to girls living in underrepresented areas. Actress and Girl Scout leader Debbie Reynolds led the charge, serving as the Honorary National Piper. This effort had four goals: that no troop would be disbanded owing to lack of leadership, that the percentage of Girl Scouts bridging to the next level would be increased, that every troop would be near its optimum size for good programming, and that the number of new troops in the least well-served areas of each local council would be increased.

Outreach overseas continued, too. In 1965, Micronesian girls in the Trust Territory of the Pacific Islands became Girl Scouts for the first time, and girls in the U.S. Territory of American Samoa were welcomed in 1968. Brownie handbooks were

LEFT
A Girl Guide and Girl Scout roller-skate in a rink, 1966.

OPPOSITE
Girl Scout Seniors are guests of NASA to view the historic *Apollo 12* moon shot at Cape Kennedy, Florida, November 14, 1969.

the civil rights movement that was sweeping the United States, turning a keen eye toward prejudice and taking action to stop it. In 1968, Girl Scout conferences called Speakouts were held to discuss prejudice and ways to eliminate it, and in 1969, the National Council launched ACTION 70, a nationwide effort to help overcome prejudice and build better relationships among all people, regardless of age, race, religion, or nationality. As an added benefit, ACTION 70 projects helped stimulate interest in Girl Scouting among girls living in urban areas, whom the movement had made a commitment to reach and serve.

The decade ended on a high note for Girl Scouts, with membership reaching nearly 4 million in 1969. That summer, Americans everywhere watched in awe as *Apollo 11* landed people on the moon, and later that year, on November 14, 130 Girl Scouts and 19 leaders from across the country viewed the *Apollo 12* moon shot firsthand in Cape Kennedy, Florida, as guests of NASA.

Throughout the soaring highs and dashing lows of the 1960s, Girl Scouts maintained a strong and reassuring presence in a country—and increasingly, a world—where unrest, chaos, and confusion frequently reigned. The movement itself offered a rock for young women in a time when everything from fashion to social mores to personal relationships seemed to be turned upside down. Here, too, young women could be assured that their efforts—even their very presence—made a difference for the greater good.

translated into Japanese for use by Girl Scouts in the Ryukyu Islands between Japan and Taiwan. Moreover, both the Brownie and Senior Girl Scout handbooks were published in Spanish and distributed to Spanish-speaking Girl Guide associations in Central and South America, as well as to Spanish-speaking Girl Scouts in the United States. The biggest event occurred in 1966, when the fourth WAGGGS world center opened in Poona (also known as Pune), India. Called Sangam, which means "coming together" in Sanskrit, it was the first world center established in Asia.

In the later 1960s, Girl Scouts fell right in with

First Ladies

Jacqueline Kennedy, beloved for her style and grace, served as National Honorary President of Girl Scouts from January 1961 to December 1963. She was a strong advocate for the arts and a champion of historic preservation—as evidenced by the White House restoration she oversaw during her years there.

When Jacqueline Kennedy's tenure as First Lady abruptly and tragically ended, Lady Bird Johnson, wife of President Lyndon B. Johnson, took over the title of National Honorary President and held it until 1969. Her passion was the beautification of the nation's cities and highways, as well as the conservation of natural resources, which was born of a lifelong love of the outdoors.

Pat Nixon became National Honorary President of Girl Scouts in 1969 with the election of her husband, Richard Nixon, as U.S. President. Pat Nixon was a staunch supporter of women's rights, becoming the first incumbent First Lady to endorse the Equal Rights Amendment and the first to appear in public in pants. She lobbied her husband hard to appoint a woman to the Supreme Court, and she called thousands of Americans to volunteerism, prompting them to carry out a variety of community services nationwide.

SIDEBAR BELOW
Lady Bird Johnson talks to a Girl Scout Junior Brownie in a White House reception room next to an oil portrait of Mrs. Herbert Hoover, 1965.

SIDEBAR BOTTOM
Pat Nixon receives a Girl Scout pin on her Stella Sloat Girl Scout uniform, circa 1970s.

Girl Scouts of all levels sing in a television studio as part of the video series *Growing Up Today*, created to help train new troop leaders. Nineteen television stations broadcast the series in 1965.

The Birthplace— a National Historic Landmark

A great honor was bestowed on the Juliette Gordon Low Birthplace and Girl Scouts' Founder on June 23, 1965, when the U.S. Department of the Interior designated the site a National Historic Landmark. It was the first building in Savannah to receive landmark status.

Adult uniforms by Stella Sloat, 1968, have two different fabrics and short or three-quarter-length sleeves.

Uniforms

In 1960, Hilda Friedman, an instructor at New York's Fashion Institute of Technology, designed a new Senior Girl Scout uniform: a tailored, two-piece, short-sleeved suit dress made of a deep jewel-tone green sharkskin cotton with an iridescent effect. The trim, classy uniform looked not unlike the smart suits that Jacqueline Kennedy made famous during the early 1960s. Accompanying the uniform was a matching "overseas" cap, with patches and hat cords to indicate special program interests.

American sportswear designer Stella Sloat reinvented the adult Girl Scout uniform in 1968, creating an easy-fitting dress with a knee-length skirt, dropped waist, short or long sleeves, and large pockets.

OPPOSITE ABOVE
A Girl Scout and a Girl Guide roast hot dogs, 1960.

OPPOSITE BELOW
A Girl Scout Cadette from Troops on Foreign Soil Troop 64 leads a group of Girl Guides from Okinawa in an American song, 1968.

BELOW
Artwork from the 1963 *Brownie Girl Scout Handbook* invites girls to paste their own picture in the reflecting pool as part of the investiture ceremony during which they become Brownies.

BOTTOM
A new Girl Scout Brownie troop's investiture ceremony

1970s

A New Future for Girls

OPPOSITE ABOVE
A Brownie and a Junior Girl Scout pose on a playground swing, 1970.

OPPOSITE BELOW
Cheryl Williams, a unit leader in Tallahassee, Florida, is surrounded by campers, 1970.

Girl Scouts has always been on the cutting edge of current issues—if not ahead of its time. The 1970s brought an enhanced focus on issues not necessarily new to Girl Scouts—such as the environment, social justice, and women's rights—and the sudden emphasis placed on them by American society proved that Girl Scout programming was right on target, anticipating—rather than reacting to—the important issues of the decade.

From the suffragette movement of the 1910s to the intensified push for equal rights in the 1970s, the place of women in society had constantly been evolving. The year 1972 saw the passing of the Equal Rights Amendment (though it has yet to be ratified into law), and throughout the 1970s women marched, lobbied, petitioned, and picketed in support of it.

The issue surfaced in music (such as Helen Reddy's "I Am Woman") and on television, where Mary Tyler Moore portrayed a successful 30-something career woman, single and self-sufficient. Reproductive rights became a hot-button issue, and divorce became a more commonly accepted option for an unhappy marriage.

With customary dignity and good sense, the Girl Scout movement did its part to support equal rights as well. Most directly, the National Board of Directors in 1977 voted to endorse the Equal Rights Amendment, but Girl Scouts also championed the cause of women by ensuring that as many girls as possible were given the chance to explore the expanding list of opportunities available to them and by giving them the skills and confidence necessary for independent, self-directed lives.

Early in the decade, a primary focus of Girl Scouts was reaching girls in isolated pockets of the United States, whether inner-city girls, daughters of migrant workers, girls in remote rural areas, or girls in other underrepresented populations. In 1970, a conference called Scouting for Black Girls was held in Atlanta, Georgia, with 150 Senior Girl Scouts and adult leaders in attendance. The aim was to explore ways to make Girl Scouting more meaningful for African American girls, who had long been members of Girl Scout troops around the country. Attendees departed with a new commitment to broaden recruitment and training efforts and ensure that the program stayed relevant to the needs of all groups, and they began to measure the extent of minority group participation. To this end, in 1972, Girl Scout membership was tracked by race for the first time.

Mexican American girls were the focus of a 1971 National Conference on Girl Scouting—Mexican-American Style. Teams of Chicano and Caucasian council representatives worked with consultants from the Mexican American community to expand membership opportunities to girls of Mexican descent. In 1973, Girl Scouts received funding from the Bureau of Indian Affairs to help extend the program to American Indian girls in eight western states. And in 1974, a three-year project was begun to connect girls in migrant communities with Girl Scout

OPPOSITE ABOVE

A group of Brownies and adult leaders march in a parade with signs and banners about recruitment, 1970.

OPPOSITE BELOW

Brownies pick up litter from around a tree planted on a city sidewalk, 1970.

BELOW

Brownie, Junior, and Cadette Girl Scouts plant a pine seedling on the lawn in front of the Utah National Guard Armory, Utah, 1970.

councils in their areas. The initiative, Girl Scouting and Migrant Communities, was funded with a private foundation grant and included the publication of a council guide, a migrant leader's guide, and a packet of program activities.

Additionally, in an effort to reach all girls, Girl Scouts arranged for paraprofessionals in inner-city, American Indian, and Mexican American communities to recruit and train neighborhood leaders.

In this decade, however, outreach was not limited only to potential Girl Scout members. Girl Scouts looked beyond membership prospects to anyone in need of friendship and support with the two-year project Hand-in-Hand: Cross-Age Interactions. Girl Scouts reached across age and economic barriers to promote intergenerational connection between young people and the elderly poor.

The environment also benefited from the attention of Girl Scouts and, increasingly, the nation at large, as the threats of air and water pollution became startlingly clear. In the fall of 1970, Eco-Action, a nationwide Girl Scout program for environmental action, was launched. Designed for girls who were already involved in environmental projects, as well as those who were not, the program strove to increase girls' awareness of the interconnectedness of everything in the environment—including themselves—and to take action to protect it.

In 1976, Girls Scouts established the Elliott Wildlife Values Project with funds from the charitable

The Legacy of Dr. Gloria D. Scott

Dr. Gloria D. Scott served as National President of Girl Scouts of the USA from 1975 to 1978 and was the first African American woman to serve as National President. She was instrumental in increasing the focus on diversity in Girl Scouts in the 1970s, and her efforts were crucial to making the face of Girl Scouting more accurately represent the face of the American population.

As a National Board member in the late 1960s, Dr. Scott observed that, despite Girl Scouts' ongoing commitment to diversity, many diverse groups were still underrepresented not only among Girl Scouts themselves but also among Girl Scout national leadership. Her efforts to change this led to the inclusion of a "critical mass" of diverse women among Girl Scout leadership, as well as to concerted efforts to increase outreach to girls of diverse populations. This resulted in several 1970s conferences that addressed diversity among Girl Scouts, such as Scouting for Black Girls in 1970 and Girl Scouting—Mexican-American Style in 1971, as well as conversations about related issues such as racism. Cutting-edge and even controversial at the time, these conferences, as

trust of preservationist Herford N. Elliott so that younger generations could further his commitment to preserving the nation's wildlife. With the objective of developing science, outdoor, and leadership skills, the program has enabled countless conservation-minded Girl Scouts to serve as stewards of the earth and leaders in the environmental movement.

The 1970s marked another period of reinvention and redefinition for the Girl Scout movement at large, as evidenced by new programs, new updates, and a fair number of "firsts." In 1972, for example, the year of the 60th anniversary of Girl Scouts, new wording was adopted for the Girl Scout Promise and Law, replacing "To do my duty to God and my country" with the updated phrase "To serve God, my country, and mankind." Older Girl Scouts were treated to a new

publication, *Runways*, in 1971, released in conjunction with the Wider Opportunities program launched in the late 1960s and full of new opportunities available nationally for older girls. In 1973, the age at which a girl could become a Girl Scout Brownie was lowered to six, introducing first-graders to the Girl Scout experience for the first time. In 1975, those same Brownies received a new magazine of their own, *Daisy*, which replaced *Brownie Reader*.

Another landmark "first" occurred in 1975, when Dr. Gloria D. Scott was elected National President. With this vote, Dr. Scott became the first African American woman to hold this office. Another African American woman, Dr. Dorothy B. Ferebee, had served as Vice President from 1969 to 1972.

Near the end of the decade, changes were made to the Girl Scout brand, with the goal of streamlining and unifying visual materials that identified Girl Scouts. The first major change was the redesign of the Girl Scout trefoil. Originally based upon the design patented by Juliette Low in 1914, it was redesigned in 1978 by designer Saul Bass. In a stylized trefoil shape, the new logo featured the silhouetted faces of three girls, symbolizing the diversity of Girl Scouts. The formal introduction of the logo at the National Council heralded the start of a three-year campaign to present to the public the contemporary Girl Scout brand. The logo, which still represents Girl Scouts today, was updated in 2010.

Then, in keeping with this effort, other visuals—such as cookie boxes and calendars—were

Dr. Scott points out, proved that Girl Scouts was "serious about diversity."

The focus on diversity led to a reexamination of nearly everything, from the way Girl Scouts was portrayed in publicity photos to its very logo. During Dr. Scott's tenure as National President, decisions were made to always include a diversity of backgrounds among girls in press photos and other images, and in 1978 a new logo, designed by Saul Bass, was unveiled. The three faces of Girl Scouts depicted in it—representing a Caucasian, an African American, and a Hispanic/Native American profile—are still the faces representing Girl Scouts today. Thanks to the passion of Dr. Scott, Girl Scouts remains a place where every girl involved can feel a sense of ownership and fairness, a sense that "this is *my* place."

also standardized, ensuring that Girl Scout troops across the country presented the same images and, ultimately, the same identity and message on all products. This represented the first time in Girl Scout history that cookie boxes, in particular, had a uniform appearance, regardless of which licensed baker produced the cookies.

The close of the 1970s also brought new and concentrated efforts to empower Girl Scouts to look forward and consider their future prospects. More opportunities were opening up to girls than ever before—especially in the realm of careers—and Girl Scouts was in a prime position to educate and excite girls about their options. Earlier in the decade, in 1970, Girl Scouts had endeavored to set girls off on the right foot early with participation in a national anti-drug-abuse workshop in Washington, D.C., at which Senior Girl Scouts and representatives of other youth organizations pledged to cooperate in fighting drug abuse.

The focus on career development intensified in later years, with the 1978 introduction of a collection of career material titled *From Dreams to Reality*. Designed for Cadette and Senior Girl Scouts, this career awareness and exploration project emphasized nonstereotyping in relation to women and careers. Additional goals included expanding girls' career potential, helping them find ways to cope with future responsibilities and solutions to the struggle of balancing a career and a family. A companion book, *Careers to Explore for Brownie and Junior Girl Scouts*,

occurred in the 1970s, the nation saw its share of struggles, and Girl Scouts faced its own challenges as well. Owing to a number of factors—including a population decrease in younger age groups, where Girl Scouting was most popular; the mobility of American families; and, ironically, an increase in the number of women who worked outside the home and had less time for volunteering—Girl Scout membership declined in this decade. These factors led to a reexamination of aspects of the Girl Scout program, and vitality was renewed, at least among the younger Girl Scout set, with the publication of a new handbook—*Worlds to Explore*. This contemporary and popular handbook addressed timely issues such as protecting the environment and the advancement of women in all areas of life. At the same time, it espoused Girl Scout program goals: deepening self-awareness, treating others with respect, developing values, and contributing to society.

But not all Girl Scout publications enjoyed a happy fate. In 1979, after careful consideration and a thorough assessment of financial viability, the beloved magazine *The American Girl* ceased publication. It had enjoyed a run spanning more than 60 years, and in that time it had become a leading teen magazine in the nation.

Despite these challenges, Girl Scouts found plenty of cause to celebrate in the 1970s. In 1976, the nation celebrated its bicentennial, and Girl Scouts around the world participated by lighting candles, or "flames of freedom," at 4:00 p.m. on March 12,

was published in 1979 to introduce younger girls to their career options, too.

Also in 1979, faculty from Harvard Business School presented the first annual corporate management seminar for Girl Scout council executives. Carried out by Harvard Business School in particular for several years, this type of seminar—focusing on the business and management aspect of running the Girl Scout organization—became a permanent feature for Girl Scouts executives.

Despite the explosion of opportunities that

the birthday of Girl Scouts. A powerful statement of longstanding Girl Scout traditions including patriotism, world understanding, and sisterhood, the act also marked a pledge of service to the nation. Girl Scouts continued to honor the 200th birthday of the United States through the Hidden Heroines program, which sought out and honored women in Girl Scouts' own communities, from the past or the present, who had not previously been recognized for their accomplishments. Identifying these women helped girls discover role models in their own neighborhoods. Girl Scouts also performed service to their communities by cleaning up parks and other public places, and by visiting patients in hospitals.

The decade also brought much honor to the memory of Founder Juliette Low, beginning in 1973, when a portrait painted of her in 1887 by London artist Sir Edward Hughes was presented to the National Portrait Gallery of the Smithsonian Institution in Washington, D.C.; it remains one of the most popular and visited portraits in the gallery. The following year, a bronze bust of Juliette Low was placed in the Georgia State Capitol Hall of Fame. At a special ceremony on her birthday that year, October 31, 1974, the bust was accepted by then–Georgia Governor Jimmy Carter. Yet another honor was bestowed on Juliette Low in 1979, when she was elected to the Women's Hall of Fame in Seneca Falls, New York.

It seems that in the 1970s, America finally caught up with Juliette Low's very progressive vision—to begin a movement that would further the

BELOW
A Girl Scout Cadette makes her Girl Scout promise, 1970.

BOTTOM
During the nation's bicentennial celebration, Girl Scouts are challenged to discover "hidden heroines" from U.S. history.

SIDEBAR BELOW
Two Girl Scout Juniors from Girl Scouts of Greater New York and adult
volunteer Sandy Jones, wearing her new Halston uniform, 1983

SIDEBAR BOTTOM
Halston poses with Frances Hesselbein, Dr. Gloria D. Scott, and other
Girl Scouts of the USA staff and adult volunteers in the new uniforms
he designed, 1978.

Uniforms

Girl Scout uniforms continued their designer appeal into the 1970s, with the Stella Sloat Senior Girl Scout design updated in 1971 to include dress slacks, a first for the official uniform ensemble. The result: an A-line tunic worn alone or as part of a pantsuit. The same look was adopted for adult Girl Scouts, at first only for casual wear but approved as an official uniform the following year.

Younger Girl Scouts enjoyed an updated look in 1973 with a new mix-and-match ensemble. The uniform components, designed for Girl Scout Brownies, Juniors, and Cadettes, included a tunic and pants, with a shorts option for Brownies and Juniors.

The adult uniform was completely refreshed in 1978 by the American couture designer Halston. The tailoring became softer, even blousy, and numerous pieces—a sage green jacket, vest, skirt, and pants, with an ivory blouse and oblong scarf that could double as a casual belt—offered women many wardrobe choices within one official uniform. The look was topped by a choice of beret or visor.

153

BELOW
Sculptor and artist Eleanor Platt works on a clay model of her Juliette Low bust, 1974.

BOTTOM
The finished bust

BOTTOM RIGHT
A program from the ceremony for the unveiling of the bust

progress of girls in America, making them capable citizens, effective leaders, and, no matter their choice of occupation in adulthood, self-sufficient and fulfilled women. As women's opportunities continued to expand in the next few decades of Girl Scouts' history, a foundation such as the one Juliette Low supplied would never be more important.

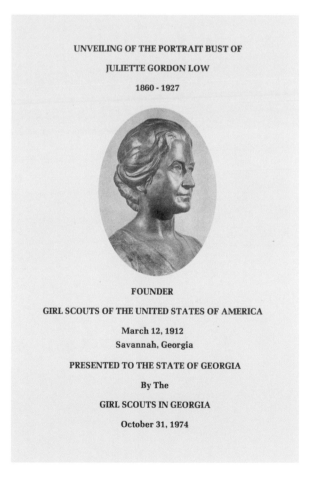

UNVEILING OF THE PORTRAIT BUST OF

JULIETTE GORDON LOW

1860 - 1927

FOUNDER

GIRL SCOUTS OF THE UNITED STATES OF AMERICA

March 12, 1912
Savannah, Georgia

PRESENTED TO THE STATE OF GEORGIA

By The

GIRL SCOUTS IN GEORGIA

October 31, 1974

Edward Hughes's portrait of Juliette Low was donated to the National Portrait Gallery by Girl Scouts of the USA in 1973.

GIRL SCOUTS *A CELEBRATION OF 100 TRAILBLAZING YEARS*

155

First Ladies

Betty Ford, wife of President Gerald Ford, became National Honorary President of Girl Scouts in 1976. An advocate of the arts and the Equal Rights Amendment, she bravely and openly faced battles with chemical dependency and breast cancer later in life, raising awareness of both and establishing herself as an important role model for the nation. It's also said that her candor about her breast cancer diagnosis spurred thousands of women to get mammogram screenings and undoubtedly saved lives.

First Lady Rosalynn Carter served as National Honorary President from 1977 to 1981. With a keen interest in women's issues and health issues, she placed her focus as First Lady on mental health. Always a humanitarian, she has continued to work on mental health reform and to support Habitat for Humanity long past her husband Jimmy Carter's presidency.

SIDEBAR BELOW
Dr. Gloria D. Scott shakes hands with Betty Ford at the White House, 1975. Dr. Scott is in Washington, D.C., for the Girl Scouts of the USA 40th National Council Session, where she is elected National President, 1975.

SIDEBAR BOTTOM
Rosalynn Carter, wife of President Jimmy Carter, stands with Junior Girl Scouts, 1980.

Girl Scout Juniors ready to deliver their Girl Scout cookies, 1973

The Julie Nixon Eisenhower Fund

Julie Nixon Eisenhower, daughter of National Honorary President Pat Nixon and a skilled needleworker, established a fund for Girl Scout services in 1970 that she fed in an exceptionally creative way: with proceeds from a crewel embroidery kit she designed and sold through *Family Circle* magazine. The Julie Nixon Eisenhower Fund was used to help extend and maintain Girl Scouting in low-income urban and rural areas, particularly through the recruiting of adult leaders.

Norman Rockwell Medals

In 1977, Norman Rockwell, the artist so famous for whimsically yet accurately capturing slices of American life, designed 12 medals for Girl Scouts. Each one was based on the ideals of the Girl Scout movement—as expressed in the Girl Scout Promise, the Girl Scout Law, and the Girl Scout motto—and the medals were issued in sets by the Franklin Mint and were available in bronze, silver, or gold.

1980s

Tradition with a Future

The 1980s were, in some ways, a fantasy decade—the nation enjoyed another cycle of boom times that ushered in landmark world events, an explosion in technology, prosperity for many Americans, and the promise of unlimited opportunities. Americans believed "you can have it all" and were encouraged to dream big.

The decade made an impact on the nation's youth, too. Girls across the United States rose before dawn one July morning in 1981 to watch the live broadcast of Princess Diana's fairy-tale wedding and were awestruck by her voluminous gown. Personal computers popped up in homes and schools. And despite the distractions of video games and MTV, Michael Jackson and Madonna, young people were keenly aware of pressing world issues: The Live Aid concert brought to light famine in Ethiopia, the space shuttle *Challenger* exploded before their eyes on classroom televisions, and they witnessed the jubilant tearing down of the Berlin Wall, signifying the collapse of communism in Eastern Europe and the dismantling of the Soviet Union.

This was a decade of significant accomplishments for women, but also new challenges. Margaret Thatcher became the first female leader of the United Kingdom, and Girl Scout alumna Sandra Day O'Connor became the first woman to take a seat on the U.S. Supreme Court. Authors Alice Walker and Toni Morrison became popular and powerful voices for black women. Across the country, more women were earning college degrees and establishing careers. Yet amid the rise of a "girls

BELOW AND FOLLOWING SPREAD
Girl Scouts participate in science activities to complete badge
requirements, circa 1980s.

SIDEBAR BELOW
Nancy Reagan at a Promise Circle event marking Girl Scouts' 75th anniversary

SIDEBAR BOTTOM
Nancy Reagan meets with Girl Scout Juniors and Cadettes at a reception.

First Ladies

Nancy Reagan, who served as First Lady and Girl Scout National Honorary President from 1981 to 1989, directly enlisted the help of Girl Scouts of the USA—in addition to other national service groups—in promoting her "Just Say No" antidrug campaign. Girl Scouts released its Contemporary Issues series, with the first title in the series addressing drug abuse, in collaboration with this effort.

can do anything!" mind-set, health and social concerns became paramount: Teen pregnancy was on the rise, and drug abuse among young people dampened many a bright future. A new disease called AIDS was mysteriously spreading to pandemic proportions. Divorce was increasingly common, resulting in more and more single-parent families and "latchkey" children.

Through it all, Girl Scouts addressed these challenges head-on, celebrated women's victories, and remained a strong draw for girls, as reflected in a rebound in membership. With a continued focus on women's issues, inclusivity, health and fitness, and the environment, Girl Scouts proved its resilience in the face of issues women could never have conceived of 70 years before.

Girl Scouts took on modern health issues, and drug abuse in particular, with the publication of the Contemporary Issues series, beginning with

BELOW
Brownies looking at "Say No to Drugs" posters, circa 1980s

BOTTOM
Tune In to Well-Being, Say No to Drugs was the first publication in the
Contemporary Issues series, 1985.

Tune In to Well-Being, Say No to Drugs. Launched
in 1985, in tandem with First Lady and Girl Scout
National Honorary President Nancy Reagan's "Just
Say No" campaign, this publication was a response
to the alarmingly high use of cocaine and crack in
the United States, increasingly a problem among
young people. Other heavy-hitting issues of the 1980s
were covered in the series as well: teen pregnancy,
child abuse, suicide, and family crises. In addition,
Contemporary Issues included topics aimed at
furthering the progress of girls: literacy, science and

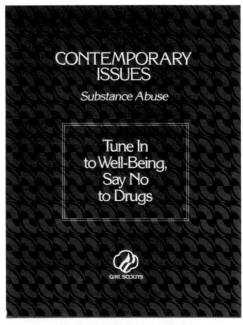

BELOW
The Gift of Water, service project publication, 1981

OPPOSITE ABOVE
Girl Scout Daisies at a playground, circa 1984

OPPOSITE BELOW
Twin Girl Scout Daisies, circa 1984

mathematics, and growing up female, as well as the evergreen issues of the environment, pluralism, and health and fitness in general.

Other efforts to set girls off on the right foot in the 1980s included the Girl Scout Career Education in Schools project, a collaboration between Girl Scout councils and school districts in 41 states to help girls explore future career options. Project Safe Time was introduced for girls whose parents were not home to care for them after school, an increasingly common issue as more mothers were in the workforce than ever before and two-income as well as single-parent families were becoming the norm.

Girl Scouts continued to shape its own movement in this decade, honing and focusing itself to be the most efficient and effective organization it could be. Part of this effort included offering management seminars for Girl Scout board president and senior executive staff conducted by well-respected leaders in the field. In 1980, the noted management authority Peter Drucker led one such seminar for Girl Scout council presidents, and the Girl Scout leadership impressed him just as much as he may have impressed them. In a *New York Times* article afterward, Drucker claimed that he considered "the Girl Scouts to be the best-managed organization around," adding, "Tough, hardworking women can do anything." No surprise, really: Girl Scouts had been proving this to be true for 70 years.

Seventy years of Girl Scouts, in and of itself, was a great landmark to celebrate, which Girl Scouts did in 1982. In keeping with their ever-present commitment to service, Girl Scouts celebrated this anniversary with a gift of service to their communities, the Gift of Water. Two options for service projects were offered in each of 10 areas, including Water Habitats; Water Safety; Water, the Arts, Our Past; and Careers in the World of Water. Girl Scouts cleaned up swamps, ponds, and riverbeds; evaluated local water sources for safety; and, in general, learned about the history and heritage of the water bodies in their communities, whether oceans, lakes, or streams.

the gift of water

girl scout action projects

First Girl Scout

An era came to an end when Daisy Gordon Lawrence, the first registered Girl Scout, died on April 26, 1982, at age 81. The niece and namesake of Juliette (Daisy) Gordon Low, Daisy Gordon signed on to the Girl Scouts at age 11 and remained active in the movement for many years. In 1958, she cowrote the book *Lady of Savannah: The Life of Juliette Low*, which was reissued in 1988.

Uniforms

Uniforms in the 1980s reflected the sporty style of the day, including T-shirts, polo shirts, and shorts. In 1980, plaid blouses topped new Cadette and Senior Girl Scout uniforms, which were virtually identical save for the color of the blouse—green plaid for Cadettes and blue plaid for Seniors.

American couture designer Bill Blass created a new seven-piece adult uniform in 1984, featuring a shirtdress with a tie belt, a boxy jacket, blouse, pants, and skirt. Topped with a jaunty beret, this uniform continued a now longstanding tradition in which a major designer re-creates the look of the Girl Scouts.

SIDEBAR BELOW
Daisy Gordon Lawrence in her adult Girl Scout uniform

SIDEBAR BOTTOM
A Girl Scout Junior helps Girl Scout Brownies with cookie deliveries, circa 1984.

SIDEBAR BELOW
Girl Scouts sell cookies from a table inside a shopping mall, circa 1983.

SIDEBAR BOTTOM
Three adult leaders in uniforms designed by Bill Blass, circa 1980s

Other uniform revisions occurred throughout the decade, with a new Junior uniform in 1985 (now featuring a T-shirt, polo shirt, and baseball cap); a new Brownie uniform in 1986 (with options including polo shirts, a jumper, pants, and shorts); and updated designs for Cadette, Senior, and adult uniforms in 1987.

Adding to the celebration, in no small part, was the fact that, after a decline in the 1970s, Girl Scout membership was enjoying a rebound—and an impressive one. Near the end of 1981, members totaled more than 2.8 million, and by 1986, that number crept upward to 2.9 million, representing the greatest increase in 18 years. By 1988, for the first time in 10 years, Girl Scouts enjoyed a membership topping 3 million.

Part of this membership boom resulted from the creation of the Daisy Girl Scout program in 1985, which extended Girl Scouting to five-year-olds. In its first year, Daisy Girl Scout membership reached 61,000, accounting for almost 3 percent of the total Girl Scout membership. The same year also saw a rise in the percentage of girls from minority populations entering Girl Scouts, accounting for 14 percent of the total membership.

No doubt this particular growth was spurred by a continued focus on multiculturalism by Girl Scouts in an effort to ever extend the Girl Scouting opportunity to all girls. Handbooks, such as the Brownie/Junior Girl Scout handbook *Worlds to Explore*, were published in Spanish. And an important report, the culmination of a study by Girl Scouts of the USA and the National Urban League, was released in 1982. Titled *The Impact of Minority Presence in Girl Scouting on White and Minority Communities*, the report revealed that increased minority participation in Girl Scouting met with overwhelming approval from not only Girl Scout membership but the general public as well. Revealing that 84 percent of the

BELOW LEFT
The Impact of Minority Presence in Girl Scouting on White and Minority Communities, 1981

BELOW RIGHT
Worlds to Explore, Spanish-language edition, 1981

BOTTOM
Girl Scouts and adult volunteers pose on the steps of the Capitol building during a tour of legislative buildings in Atlanta, Georgia, with Governor Joe Frank Harris as part of the Avon Leadership Conference, 1985.

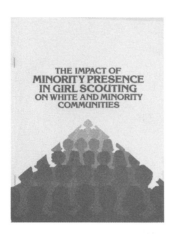

American public deemed Girl Scouting "good" or "excellent," the study also showed that fully half the American population had been involved in Girl Scout activities, whether directly or through a friend or family member.

In 1983, a multicultural conference, Women Are History: Women of Color, Past, Present, and Future, was held at the newly dedicated Edith Macy Conference Center, built on the original site dedicated to Girl Scouts in 1926. The Women Are History conference was designed to help Girl Scouts collaborate with organizations of women of color in their own communities, thereby developing and strengthening existing relationships with such groups. Furthering this effort, in 1986, a conference funded by the cosmetic company Avon Products Inc. sought to strengthen self, family, and community ties, especially among African American, Hispanic, and Asian girls and women. The participants, registered as teams of Senior Girl Scouts and adult leaders, collaborated on a council plan for outreach to local minority communities.

One tangible result of all these efforts was that, in 1987, Girl Scout membership among minority populations rose 5 percent, a record increase. The face of Girl Scouting in America continued to change, reflecting the actual population of the United States and ensuring that Girl Scouts kept its vow to be accessible to every girl, everywhere. It's particularly fitting that, in 1984, at a luncheon celebrating the 72nd birthday of Girl Scouts, President Ronald Reagan announced, "When we celebrate the Girl Scouts, we celebrate America."

America celebrated a very specific Girl Scout that same year—Kathryn Sullivan, an active adult member of Girl Scouts and an astronaut, who was among the crew aboard NASA's space shuttle *Challenger* on its first flight. On October 11, 1984, she became the first woman to walk in space. No fewer than 21 astronauts at that time had been Girl Scouts. When Juliette Low envisioned a movement that would break down barriers for girls, perhaps she imagined women accomplishing just such feats as this.

Unfortunately, the thrill of sending women into space was accompanied by tragedy. Just two years later, in 1986, the *Challenger* exploded during takeoff for another space mission, this time claiming the lives of everyone aboard, including Christa McAuliffe, a schoolteacher and Girl Scout alumna. McAuliffe had always demonstrated true Girl Scout courage and ambition, and to this day she stands as an inspiring and unforgettable—if heartbreaking—role model for many girls.

Amid the highs and lows of the decade, Girl Scouts continued to evolve to meet the needs of the organization and the realities of modern times. In 1982, the first annual Leader's Day recognized the contributions of adult leaders nationwide, and in 1983, the ultimate Girl Scout leader—Founder Juliette Low—was honored when a federal office building in Savannah was named for her, just the second federal building in the nation to be named after a woman.

Edith Macy Conference Center

In 1980, ground was broken for the Edith Macy Conference Center in Westchester County, New York, on the original Camp Edith Macy site donated to Girl Scouts in 1926. The building, a year-round conference center and training facility, was dedicated two years later, in 1982.

Thanks to the fund-raising efforts of Metropolitan Life Insurance Company president John J. Creedon, as well as contributions from Girl Scouts and Girl Scout volunteers alike, the resulting building was a gem: Built of wood, stone, and glass, the conference center was both modern and entirely fitting in a natural setting. Well used by Girl Scouts today, and often rented to outside groups for special gatherings, the Edith Macy Conference Center comprises five conference rooms, a 200-seat auditorium, a resource room, a dining room, and a cozy "commons" area, as well as a Friendship Room designed for quiet reflection. Near the conference center lie three residential buildings with a total of 46 guest rooms.

A second major phase of development was completed in

An aerial view of the Edith Macy Conference Center, a year-round, residential, multipurpose conference and training facility on the grounds of the Edith Macy Girl Scout National Center, 1982.

The entrance to the Edith Macy Conference Center, 1982

A plaque for the Outdoor Education Center, 1988

1988, when the Outdoor Education Center was added to the site, offering year-round outdoor programming and featuring the Camp of Tomorrow, a complex of four state-of-the-art meeting and lodging rooms designed to minimize environmental impact—complete with solar heat, minimum-impact design, and even composting toilets. In October 1988, the Outdoor Education Center was renamed the John J. Creedon Center in honor of the man who headed up the fund-raising campaign for the Edith Macy Conference Center.

Frances Hesselbein, National CEO

Frances Hesselbein, founding president/CEO and now chair of the board of governors of the Leader to Leader Institute (formerly the Peter F. Drucker Foundation for Nonprofit Management), served as National CEO of Girl Scouts from July 1976 to January 1990. She is considered an iconic nonprofit leader and a "guru" of the American business community. Peter Drucker hailed Ms. Hesselbein as one of the country's best leaders, saying that "Frances Hesselbein could manage any company in America."

During her fourteen-year tenure as CEO of Girl Scouts of the USA, she transformed Girl Scouting by:

- Bringing the importance of helping every girl reach her potential to the forefront
- Abandoning outdated practices and organizational charts in favor of innovative systems that established clear performance measures and were no longer top-down
- Helping membership to reach its highest level in history—including

SIDEBAR BELOW
Making the Girl Scout sign and saying the Girl Scout Promise, newly invested National Honorary President Nancy Reagan joins National President Mrs. Orville Freeman, left, and National Executive Director Frances Hesselbein, right.

SIDEBAR BOTTOM
Frances Hesselbein, circa 1980s

In 1984, the words of the Girl Scout Promise were revised to embrace an emphasis on nonsexist language—specifically, the phrase "To serve God, my country, and mankind" was changed to "To serve God and my country, to help people at all times." In 1985, the Troops on Foreign Soil program (TOFS) was renamed USA Girl Scouts Overseas (USAGSO). New Brownie and Junior Scout handbooks were offered in 1986, with new handbooks for Cadette and Senior Girl Scouts to follow in 1987.

In 1984, for the first time since 1948, Girl Scouts of the USA hosted a World Conference, its 25th. It was held in Tarrytown, New York, with 417 Girl Scout and Girl Guide delegates from 92 nations. In 1987, Girl Scouts of the USA established a National Historic Preservation Center (NHPC) for the preservation and promotion of Girl Scout history. The National Historic Preservation Center opened at National Headquarters in New York in 1989.

The year 1987 also brought another landmark celebration: the 75th anniversary of Girl Scouting, celebrated under the theme "Tradition with a Future." March 12, 1987, saw Girl Scouts around the globe participate in Promise Circle ceremonies, which began at exactly 4:00 p.m. in their respective time zones, when they gathered to recite the Girl Scout Promise. In Washington, D.C., 2,000 Girl Scouts participated in a national Promise Circle event at the John F. Kennedy Center for the Performing Arts, and they planted an elm tree on the Ellipse behind the White House the following day. The U.S. Postal Service

a 300 percent increase in membership among girls from diverse population groups

In January 1998, Ms. Hesselbein was awarded the Presidential Medal of Freedom, the United States' highest civilian honor. The award recognized her leadership as Chief Executive Officer of Girl Scouts as well as her role as founding president of the Peter F. Drucker Foundation for Nonprofit Management.

Ms. Hesselbein has authored various articles and books, including *Hesselbein on Leadership*. She has served on multiple boards of directors—of for-profit and nonprofit organizations—and is widely recognized for her contributions to the nonprofit sector.

Girl Scout Gold Award

In 1980, the Girl Scout Gold Award for Girl Scout Seniors replaced First Class as the highest recognition in Girl Scouting. For Girl Scout Cadettes, the Girl Scout Silver Award became the highest honor. For both age levels, the requirements for earning such an award included completion of projects in leadership, career exploration, and service, as well as demonstrated ability in goal setting, planning, putting values into action, and community involvement.

SIDEBAR
The Girl Scout Gold Award

BELOW
Girl Scout Juniors on a swing, circa 1980s

issued a commemorative Girl Scout stamp to honor the anniversary, and a Girl Scout exhibit was unveiled at the Smithsonian Institution's National Museum of American History in Washington, D.C., featuring vintage uniforms, photographs, and memorabilia. During the time of its display, from March 12 to August of that year, it drew more than 4 million visitors. On a more local note, Juliette Low and her achievements were also celebrated in Savannah during its Georgia Day festivities in February of that year. Town Hall meetings with a woman representing Juliette Low were held in schools all over Chatham County, and a parade through downtown Savannah was held that featured

5,000 costumed students, uniformed Girl Scouts, and "Juliette Low" leading them all in a Model T Ford.

In 1988, Girl Scouts opened the Camp of Tomorrow at the Edith Macy Conference Center; it offered a year-round program focused on camping and environmental and wildlife education, as well as on training for girls and adults. Later that year, the Camp of Tomorrow was renamed the John J. Creedon Center to honor the man who headed the committee that raised the funds for the Edith Macy Conference Center.

Also in 1988, a Girl Scout Center for Innovation opened in Southern California, with the purpose of designing and field-testing methods of extending Girl Scouting even further to minority populations. The projects it promoted focused on preventing teen pregnancy, valuing differences, and bringing Head Start "graduates" into the Girl Scout Daisy program.

But amid all these innovations, tough decisions were required to keep the movement going forward efficiently and cost-effectively. In 1981, for example, *Daisy* magazine published its last issue. National President Jane Freeman admitted that the decision to end the magazine had been difficult but necessary due to increasing publication costs. In 1982, the Rockwood Girl Scout National Center in Potomac, Maryland, was sold after it was determined that keeping it open was no longer economically feasible. The site is now owned by the Maryland–National Capital Park and Planning Commission and is available for outdoor

Take the Lead

Campfire songs aren't the only songs made famous by Girl Scouts. In 1988, a Girl Scout rap song, "Take the Lead," won a gold award in the 1988 Mercury Competition for promotional materials. Featured in a radio public service announcement, the Girl Scout song won one of the 50 awards that were distributed among 900 contestants.

Take the Lead

I'm a young girl
GROWING UP TOO FAST!
Doing lots of things
THAT JUST WON'T LAST!
Learning all the slang
And hip things too,
Til I found something better to do.
And now I'll share it with you!

TAKE THE LEAD!

A lady walks in to my life
And says,
"Say girl, want to know what's right?
I can show you how to reach for the stars,
Take hold of your life and you'll go far."
I say, "Hey what's this all about?"
She smiles and says,
"I'm a Girl Scout."
"A Girl Scout? A Girl Scout, you say?
How can you show me the way?"
Then she begins to share with me,
All the things a Girl Scout can be.
Be an astronaut or a president,
Spread your wings. Experiment!
Go swimming, camping, even hiking!
Have fun with your friends while you are biking!

CHORUS:
TAKE, TAKE, TAKE THE LEAD!
GIRL SCOUTS IS ALL YOU NEED TO
TAKE THE LEAD,
GIRL SCOUTS IS ALL YOU NEED!

When drugs are all around,
Stand your ground!
When they offer it to you,
Turn it down!
There are things you can do
That won't harm you!

Learn all about jobs,
And stay in school!

REPEAT CHORUS

The one I like to emulate.
YES!
My Girl Scout leader.
WOW!
She's great!
We've grown so close these past few years,
She's shared my hopes and eased my fears.
I can't believe she's now my friend—
My leader.
YEAH!
I really need her!
Together we dream of travels worldwide,
Meeting Girl Scouts and Girl Guides.
When I think of this, I beam with pride
That this leader stands by my side.

REPEAT CHORUS

Lead a patrol!
Catch control,
And Girl Scouts
WILL HELP YOU GROW!
Peer pressure is nothing to worry about,
If you join us and become a Girl Scout!
Take charge of your life,
We'll help with all you need.
Then all you have to do
is stand up and
TAKE THE LEAD!
GET IT?
YEAH!

REPEAT CHORUS TWICE

TAKE THE LEAD!

Lyrics to JUCs' rap song by Carr'Mel F. White

BELOW LEFT
A National Center West patch

BELOW
National Center West, Ten Sleep, Wyoming

BOTTOM
Girl Scout Brownies have fun on a tire swing, circa 1980s.

programming for Girl Scouts as well as for the enjoyment of the general public.

In addition, after careful study and consideration, National Center West, the national outdoor center located in Ten Sleep, Wyoming, was also closed, but in keeping with Girl Scouts' commitment to conservation, the property was sold to the Nature Conservancy, ensuring the protection and preservation of the environment as well as the archaeological sites and fragile geological features located there.

On the brink of a new decade, Girl Scouts kept their focus forward, closing the 1980s with a commitment to "Leadership in Action," established at the 1989 National Program Conferences. Eight critical issues were identified for future action: all-girl organizations, pluralism, community, the environment, taking the lead for a better world, innovation in action, international aspects of Girl Scouting, and leadership. Also in 1989, Girl Scouts of the USA established the 21st Century Endowment Fund, intended to enhance program opportunities and services to councils and ensure that Girl Scout endeavors would continue well throughout the century—and beyond.

Girl Scouts with a martial arts instructor, circa 1980s

BOTTOM
Girl Scout Cadettes in their life vests carry a canoe, 1980.

1990s

Where Girls Grow Strong

National Girl Scout Reunion

85th

ANNIVERSARY

1912 Girl Scouts 1997

OPPOSITE

Janet Reno sits with five Girl Scouts, one from each age level.

A decade hurtling forward—that was the 1990s. In just a few short years, massive advancements were made in technology, in particular, that would transform the way people all over the world communicated and managed their affairs. In 1996, almost no one had a cell phone; by 1999, almost *everyone* did. Mid-decade, people were just gaining access to the Internet; by the end of the 1990s, the world was so dependent on it—and computer systems in general—that fear surrounding a Y2K crash was palpable. A dot-com bubble began growing that was destined to burst.

This was a decade of wars—in the Persian Gulf, Bosnia, and Somalia—but also peace, as apartheid ended in South Africa and the Irish Republican Army and Great Britain declared a truce. It was a decade of unprecedented economic expansion in the United States, but also new threats, as the Oklahoma City bombing proved terrorists could be U.S.-born and the Columbine shooting proved that violence could reach even a school.

Young people, though keenly aware of these headlines, enjoyed a new sense of counterculture individualism that permeated every aspect of their lives. Fringe music genres like grunge, alternative, hip-hop, and punk went mainstream, and the rule of fashion was "anything goes," allowing flannel shirts to coexist with vintage couture. Women were making strides like never before, as the 1990s saw a record number of women becoming CEOs and gaining high-ranking government positions—such as Secretary of State Madeleine Albright, Attorney General Janet Reno, and Justice Ruth Bader Ginsburg, the second woman to sit on the Supreme Court. "Girl power!" became a rallying cry.

It certainly was the cry of Girl Scouts, who kept in step with every aspect of the decade's progress. With an overarching theme of promoting self-esteem, Girl Scouts plunged into opportunities for exploring science and technology, sports and fitness, and gender equity. Their ever-present focus on the environment and multiculturalism served them well in a rapidly shrinking world that was becoming shockingly aware of humans' impact on the earth. Like the vintage styles hanging in modern girls' closets, Girl Scouts' enduring principles were not out of place in the digital age.

Girl Scouts also ensured that girls had no shortage of things to do—away from computer screens and out in the wide outdoors. Through a variety of Wider Opportunities, the 1990s found Girl Scouts just about everywhere, exploring their deepest interests as well as the far reaches of the world. For example, girls literally got their feet wet exploring the marvels of aquatic life from the Great Lakes to the Gulf of Mexico. They explored the lakes bordering Canada in canoes and backpacked in the Sierra Nevada. They explored careers in art and architecture, theater and therapy, physics and engineering. Some even ventured overseas, living with host families in foreign countries or visiting WAGGGS centers.

Girl Scouts also made a global impact through USA Girl Scouts Overseas (formerly known as Troops on Foreign Soil). No matter where in the world Girl Scout troops were located, they were serving the people around them. In Dakar, Senegal, for example, Brownie Girl Scouts collected recyclable items such as bottles, jars, and newspapers, which were redeemed for milk and infant formula, to benefit children at an orphanage there, while their Junior Girl Scout sisters collected food and clothing. In Guantánamo Bay, Cuba, Girl Scouts organized a Thanksgiving Day potluck dinner for Marine personnel stationed there. Girl Scouts–Bermuda explored the natural environment of their island home while organizing a beach cleanup, and girls involved in Girl Scouts–Jakarta sponsored fitness events, including an 80-kilometer hike up a volcano and back.

Discovering their own regions as well as far-flung locales, Girl Scouts were out in the world *doing* in an age when it was increasingly tempting to passively surf the Internet for hours.

A major initiative of Girl Scouts in 1990 was Right to Read, a national service project aimed at improving literacy among members of Girl Scouts' own communities who may have lacked the basic skills necessary to read signs, fill out forms, interpret critical documents, or simply enjoy reading for pleasure. Girl Scouts planned service activities for Right to Read with three points in mind: reading to help yourself, reading to help your friends, and reading to help at home and in the community. Nearly

4 million Girl Scouts—girls and adult volunteers—as well as National Honorary President Barbara Bush were involved in this project

Health was another important topic for Girl Scouts in the 1990s, beginning with the health of the planet. In 1992, Girl Scouts celebrated its 80th anniversary by launching a nationwide environmental service project, Girl Scouts Care for the Earth. In keeping with the nation's heightened awareness of recycling and sustainable development, Girl Scouts embarked on projects to protect the earth's natural resources, environmental cleanup and tree planting projects, water management projects, and recycling efforts. In 1997, Girl Scouts were given the chance to explore national resource issues and careers in conservation and wildlife through Linking Girls to the Land, a project funded jointly by the Elliot Wildlife Values Project, the U.S. Forest Service, the Environmental Protection Agency, and several other related government agencies. And in 1999, the Elliott Wildlife Values Project also provided grants for the EarthPACT Project, again with the mission of engaging girls in environment-related career exploration through hands-on activities and internships.

Girls' own health and fitness came next, with the 1993 Be Your Best campaign. A new title in the Contemporary Issues series was released— *Developing Health and Fitness: Be Your Best*—and with it a fitness video hosted by Olympic gold medalist Janet Evans that featured Girl Scouts doing exercises and discussing health topics. The

SIDEBAR TOP
Honorary National President Barbara Bush and Girl Scouts, 1990s

SIDEBAR BOTTOM
Honorary National President Hillary Rodham Clinton greets a Senior
Girl Scout, 1997.

First Ladies

Barbara Bush accepted the position of National Honorary President from 1989 to 1993, but perhaps her greatest contribution to Girl Scouts came in 1990, when she helped the movement launch the national Girl Scout literacy project Right to Read. Through this program, nearly 4 million Girl Scouts strove to hone their own literacy skills and helped ensure that many other Americans did so as well.

First Lady Hillary Rodham Clinton was next in line as National Honorary President, serving from 1993 to 2001. She hosted a White House Conference on Philanthropy at which a Girl Scout philanthropist patch was unveiled, and also served as an excellent role model for women in leadership. Not only the most empowered and politically powerful First Lady to that point, Girl Scout alumna Clinton later served as a U.S. senator and is currently the secretary of state.

BELOW
Developing Health and Fitness, 1992

BOTTOM
Welcome to Girl Scouting/Bienvenidos a Girl Scouting was published
in 1990 for Girl Scout Daisy adult volunteers.

overall Be Your Best campaign—a national service
project—encouraged Girl Scouts to promote healthy
living, keeping fit, and eating right, among other
topics, in their communities. This endeavor also led
to the first annual Girl Scout Be Your Best Day in
1995, celebrated on March 14. Girl Scouts nationwide
encouraged friends and family members to do
something that day that exemplified "being your
best," and they enjoyed the support of celebrity
spokespersons such as 14-year-old tennis star Venus
Williams and NASA astronaut Tamara Jernigan, as
well as teen television personalities Tatyana M. Ali
(*Fresh Prince of Bel-Air*) and Mayim Bialik (*Blossom*).

On a side note: In this highly health-conscious
era, it's worth mentioning that even Girl Scout
cookies were not exempt from reexamination. Two
new varieties were introduced in 1994—a Cinnamon
Oatmeal Raisin bar and an iced oatmeal raisin cookie
called Snaps—that boasted low-fat or fat-free contents.

In keeping with the health and fitness focus—
but also with a nod toward gender equity—sports
programs for Girl Scouts abounded in the 1990s. In
1996, for example, a new program called Sports +
Girls = A Winning Team was designed to support
girls' interest and participation in sports while
creating new ways to deliver the Girl Scout program.
This initiative was accompanied by a *Girls and
Sports Extra* supplement that was published six
times a year and included in *Sports Illustrated for
Kids.* Other sports initiatives included a golf program
through partnership with the Ladies Professional

Golf Association and the U.S. Golf Association, and a Leadership in Sports Institute, which was held at the Edith Macy Conference Center. There, Senior Girl Scouts participated in workshops on sports ethics, sports careers, sports psychology, and personal fitness and nutrition.

In 1997, the first national GirlSports event was held for Senior Girl Scouts at Converse College in South Carolina. Providing sports activities, games, and workshops, this event hosted nearly 200 Senior Girl Scouts from 44 states. This also led to the implementation of Sports Days, a revamp of Sports + Girls = A Winning Team that featured council-designed events promoting sports, health, and fitness for girls. Another project, GirlSports 2000, was launched in 1998 with a focus on the participation—rather than the competition—aspect of sports. It also spurred Girl Scouts nationwide to get in shape for the coming millennium by scheduling troop or group sports events every day throughout 1999. Their cheering section was top-notch: Seven women sports stars, from Olympic gold medalists to professional sports celebrities, were spokespeople and role models for this initiative—alumnae Girl Scouts all.

The 1990s also saw Girl Scouts continue their commitment to diversity, and to reaching all girls in the United States, which they did in unprecedented ways. In doing so, they explored underrepresented regions, first through an effort to introduce Girl Scout activities during and after school hours through Girl Scouting in the School Day. With this program, Girl Scouting could be offered to even more girls, in isolated rural regions as well as heavily populated urban areas.

Reaching another underrepresented region of the United States, Girl Scouts opened a Center for Innovation in Appalachia in 1992, through which Girl Scouts could serve girls in West Virginia, Kentucky, Tennessee, and Virginia. Its features included a Housing Authority Drop-In Center serving about 250 displaced families, a before-school mentoring program for middle and high school girls called the Breakfast Club, and a summer program for girls. Nationwide, Girl Scouts also extended a hand to girls whose mothers were incarcerated, offering them a chance to bond with their mothers through a program called Girl Scouts Beyond Bars, a 1992 collaboration with the National Institute of Justice. This program facilitated mother-daughter prison visits, offered parent education and transitioning programs for the mothers, and provided education and activities for the girls, with the hope of easing the traumatic effects of separation and helping the girls develop resilience and life skills.

Girl Scouts kept working to develop better programs for the diverse populations they were already serving, too. In 1990, for example, a Center for Innovation was opened in Texas to better extend Girl Scout participation to Hispanic girls. Out of this center came the publication of a 1993 resource guide, *Spotlight on Success: Serving the Mexican-American Community*, which described the many projects and initiatives coming from the center and evaluated their effectiveness. Additionally, throughout the 1990s, Girl Scout materials, from print publications to informational videos, were increasingly translated into Spanish. A 1997 bilingual resource, *Welcome to Girl Scouting/Bienvenidos a Girl Scouting*, was published as part of an initiative called Building Inclusion Through Language that stemmed from a Spanish language resources conference (also called Inclusion Through Language) held in 1996 at the Edith Macy Conference Center.

Earlier in the decade, Girl Scouts published *Focus on Ability: Serving Girls with Special Needs* to improve services for Girl Scouts with disabilities, and a longtime focus on recruiting girls in American Indian populations was continued with the guide *Girl Scouting and the American Indian Community*. Several studies and conferences conducted by Girl Scouts led to more education about, and more programs tailored for, diverse populations. These included the 1993 *Strength in Diversity* study, as well as the 1995 program Unity in Diversity, a series of eight training events designed to help Girl Scout executive staff better value all aspects of diversity. In 1996, a publication titled *A Bridge to the Future: The History of Diversity in Girl Scouting* was released, documenting Girl Scouts' longtime commitment to serving girls from all racial and ethnic backgrounds. This endeavor to embrace multiculturalism was also reflected in a 1999 Brownie/Junior Girl Scout program, Girl Scouts Go Global!, which engaged younger Girl Scouts in increasing their awareness

of current global issues and understanding their connections to the world through culture and heritage, among other topics.

The result of all these initiatives? Girl Scouts enjoyed steadily increasing membership numbers throughout the 1990s, ending the decade 3.6 million Girl Scouts strong. Though that figure alone is impressive, it doesn't begin to tell the stories of girls from all walks of life, all regions, and all cultures who themselves were made stronger by Girl Scouting.

Indeed, making girls strong was Girl Scouts' contribution to a decade focused on "girl power" in America, and the movement did so through many initiatives focused on the empowerment of girls. The first of these, a symposium called Today's Girls, Tomorrow's Leaders, which was cosponsored by the American Association of University Women, was held in 1992. Examining the needs of girls and how they were being met in a single-sex environment, the symposium attracted more than 150 educators, youth service workers, psychologists, and members of the press. The AAUW partnered with Girl Scouts again in 1994 to develop a gender equity training module titled Ensuring Unbiased Behavior in an All-Girl Environment.

Ever keeping up with the times—and the changing needs of girls—Girl Scouts also marked the decade with a series of significant studies that not only informed program changes but also illuminated the interests and concerns of a new generation of girls. Conducted by Louis Harris & Associates, *The*

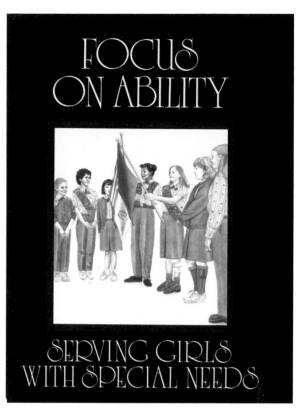

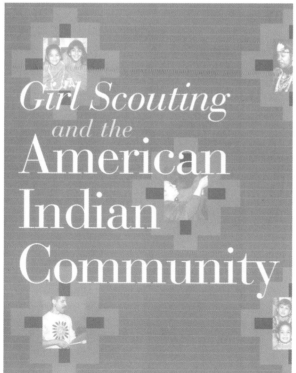

Pax Lodge

In 1991, Pax Lodge opened in London, replacing Olave House to become the newest WAGGGS world center. Providing facilities for international trainings, seminars, and conferences, Pax Lodge joined the other WAGGGS world centers in welcoming Girl Scouts and Girl Guides from all over the world.

Girl Scouts Survey on the Beliefs and Moral Values of America's Children and *Girl Scouts: Who We Are, What We Think* provided insight into the realities of contemporary girls and young women and also revealed Girl Scouts to be a highly valued, vital, and relevant movement important for all girls, regardless of where and how they lived. Further studies followed, overwhelmingly revealing that Girl Scouting gave girls the ability to work well with others, gain self-confidence, and develop a social conscience. Significantly, Girl Scouts was also giving girls the skills to become successful leaders in the future.

Confident that the movement was on the right track, Girl Scouts went to work preparing its young members for lives and careers in a rapidly changing world. The first item on the list for the organization was to establish a presence on the World Wide Web. Girl Scouts achieved this in 1996 with the launch of www.girlscouts.org on February 1. Featuring news highlights, Girl Scout history, links to council sites, and Girl Scout merchandise, the site quickly enjoyed frequent visitors—and still does. The following year saw the addition of a new website, Just for Girls (www.girlscouts.org/girls), an interactive site where Girl Scouts ages 6 to 17 could swap information and their thoughts with others. Immensely popular was a feature called "Ask Dr. M," where girls could seek advice from a Girl Scouts of the USA staff member who was also a developmental psychologist, and her daughter, a Girl Scout Cadette. Today, the Just for Girls site can be found online.

By 1998, Girl Scouts of the USA had laid the groundwork for an Online Council Network featuring an exclusive Internet link between Girl Scouts councils and Girl Scouts of the USA National Headquarters. It's also fitting that, the same year, a Technology badge was introduced for Junior Girl Scouts. The requirements? Well, they could be found online.

Next on the Girl Scout agenda was setting up programs and initiatives offering Girl Scouts hands-on experience with contemporary topics and cutting-edge career opportunities. Happily, there was no shortage of outside corporations and organizations that willingly stepped up to help Girl Scouts achieve this goal. Grants were provided throughout the decade to support Girl Scouts in assisting people in need, preventing youth violence, and establishing an adult-to-youth mentoring program. Other grants supported leadership development, multicultural recruitment programs, and literacy initiatives. The

Uniforms

The fashion of the day was "anything goes," and Girl Scout uniforms in the 1990s possessed a certain amount of fun. While the adult uniforms introduced in 1990 remained as stylish as ever—with a more formal tailored option as well as a more casual uniform for active wear—girls' uniforms, especially for younger Girl Scouts, reflected the individualistic style of the day.

Take, for example, the Daisy and Brownie Girl Scout uniforms introduced in 1993. Part of a complete program update for the younger Girl Scouts, they featured new colors, vibrant prints, and modern styling. Chambray shirts and T-shirts with bright screen prints became the norm, giving girls a consistent yet playful look.

The 1994 Salute to Girl Scout Style fashion show in New York City marked the debut of a new Junior Scout uniform incorporating the playful, casual aspects of the younger Girl Scouts' gear. Bold styling, bright colors, and coordinated separates— including solid-color or multicolor flower-print leggings—updated the look for this age group.

The uniform update became complete in 1995 with new Cadette and Senior Girl Scout uniform

BELOW
A Girl Scout makes her Girl Scout Promise, circa 1990s.

BOTTOM
A Girl Scout Brownie, circa 1990s

SIDEBAR
A Girl Scout views memorabilia at a visit to the National Historic Preservation Center, 2009.

components, which included sweatshirts and baseball caps.

Uniforms of the past were also celebrated during the 1990s. The aforementioned Salute to Girl Scout Style featured a parade of Girl Scout uniforms throughout the decades, and also in 1994, a book of paper dolls—*On My Honor*—featured dozens of historically accurate Girl Scout uniforms from 1912 to 1928 as well as paper dolls depicting none other than Juliette Low and Lou Henry Hoover.

For All the Girls

On March 11, 1994, a permanent exhibit was installed at the Girl Scout National Historic Preservation Center in New York City. Titled ". . . for all the girls," the exhibit displays vintage uniforms, publications, and memorabilia.

OPPOSITE
Brownie Girl Scouts crowd together for a portrait on the grounds of
Pax Lodge, 1991.

BELOW
A Girl Scout Daisy, circa 1990s

Elks Foundation awarded college scholarships to
selected Girl Scout Gold Award recipients.

Girls were exposed to opportunities in science
with support from the National Science Foundation
(and other organizations), which paired Girl Scout
troops with local science museums to encourage
the discovery of nature, animal life, physics, the
planets, and other scientific topics. And the Lockheed
Martin Corporate Foundation provided a Science

Thin Mint Ice Cream

There might not be a much better
combination than Girl Scout Thin Mint
cookies and ice cream—a fact that
was not lost on the Dreyer's Grand
Ice Cream company in 1998, when it
introduced Girl Scout Thin Mint Cookie
Ice Cream. The limited-edition treat
was offered nationally (and under the
brand name Edy's east of the Rocky
Mountains) from March through
August of that year.

Connie Matsui

The year 1999 brought another first for Girl Scouts when Connie L. Matsui was elected National President, becoming the first Asian American woman to hold that position. A longtime Girl Scout volunteer, in her "day job" Matsui was vice president of planning and resource development at IDEC Pharmaceuticals, a company that developed therapies for people with cancer and autoimmune disorders.

Career Exploration Fund, providing grants for programs exposing girls to careers in science, math, engineering, and technology.

Other funding went to practical programs for mindful girls, offering publications such as *Girl Scouts Money Smarts* (National Endowment for Financial Education), *Spotlight on Success: Guide for Community Cultivation* (Kellogg Foundation), *Girl Scouts Against Smoking* (Robert Wood Johnson Foundation), and *Learning About Government* (Ford Foundation). Even the Kappa Delta Sorority (among others) got involved, naming Girl Scouts of the USA as its official philanthropic organization. In doing so, it linked Girl Scout councils with Kappa Delta chapters for service projects, recognizing the organizations' shared commitment to values such as honesty, integrity, and friendship.

Preparing girls for the challenges of the 21st century was the focus of an end-of-the-millennium initiative called Girl Power!, produced in conjunction with the U.S. Department of Health and Human Services. The program included two age-appropriate booklets—the Girl Scout Juniors' *Girl Power! How to Get It* and the Cadettes' *Girl Power! Keep It Going*—and the opportunity to earn a Girl Power! patch for completion.

Always looking for ways to improve the movement and keep it strong, current, and relevant, Girl Scouts engaged in many internal changes in the 1990s as well. Physically, the organization moved its National Headquarters to its current location, at 420

Fifth Avenue in New York City, after a study on its space needs and financial options.

Other updates took place as well, reflecting concerns of the time and leading the Girl Scout movement to take strong and sometimes daring stands for what it believed in. One of the most significant was a revision to the wording of the spoken Girl Scout Promise in 1993, this time making it more flexible for girls of all cultures and religious (or nonreligious) backgrounds by allowing another word or phrase to be substituted for *God*. Later in the decade, the Girl Scout Law was also revised to contain wording that was more contemporary and comprehensive. In 1994, Girl Scouts explicitly stated its own beliefs and stances with the publication of the book *What We Stand For*, which clarified the movement's principles and stated its official positions on a number of key issues.

In 1995, a Girl Scout Executive Director Certification Program was launched. The program gave Girl Scout councils a standardized way to assess the qualifications of their executive directors, both current and future.

Finally, in 1999, Girl Scouts launched a new brand image campaign—Girl Scouts: Where Girls Grow Strong—through which it sought to communicate unity of purpose throughout the organization and to the public. After examination of the many studies conducted throughout the decade, what became apparent was that the term "Girl Scouts," in and of itself, was a strong enough

identifier to powerfully and positively convey the impact the movement had not only on girls but also the community—and, truly, the nation.

Girl Scouts ended the decade—and the millennium—with the assurance that it was making a tremendous impact on girls, on the place of women in the nation, and, as part of the global Girl Scouting movement, on the entire world. It wasn't a bad way to head into the 21st century and the challenges—and multiplying opportunities—it would bring.

2000 AND BEYOND

Girls Lead the Way

January 1, 2000, was celebrated around the
world as the beginning of a new millennium.
Intermingled with the excitement of a
modern turn of the century were the promise of
unprecedented economic good times and the thrill
of technological possibility—buoyed by the fact that,
with the stroke of midnight that New Year's Eve, the
Y2K threat fizzled away.

But not all hopes came to fruition. In reality,
the first decade of the 2000s set off a financial roller
coaster as the dot-com boom busted, the housing
bubble burst, and, toward the end of the decade, a
Wall Street crash led to a deep recession and financial
instability for millions of Americans. The sense
of peace Americans had enjoyed in the 1990s was
shattered on September 11, 2001, with terrorist attacks
on New York City and the Pentagon that rattled
Americans to the core. This event also launched
the United States and global allies into wars in
Afghanistan and Iraq that continued into the next
decade. Natural disasters such as the 2004 tsunami
in the Indian Ocean and 2005's Hurricane Katrina,
which devastated the Gulf Coast, renewed concerns
about natural disasters and climate change.

But not all was gloomy in this decade—far from
it. In 2008, Barack Obama became the first African
American president, and in so doing introduced
Girl Scouts to its first African American National
Honorary President, Michelle Obama. Technology
advanced at a remarkable speed, opening up new
avenues for communication, enjoyed especially

First Lady Michelle Obama agrees to serve as Honorary National President of the Girl Scouts, October 7, 2009. Pictured, from left to right, are Connie Lindsey, Sharon Pearce, Girl Scouts from the Nation's Capital Council, President Obama, Michelle Obama, and Kathy Cloninger.

First Ladies

Laura Bush became First Lady—and Girl Scout National Honorary President—upon the inauguration of her husband, George W. Bush, as president in 2001 and served in that role until 2009. In that time—and well beyond—she has been a strong advocate for the movement, appearing at numerous Girl Scout events long after her time as First Lady ended.

Michelle Obama stepped up to the honor next, becoming Girl Scouts' first African American National Honorary President, and she too is taking a very active role in the movement. In keeping with her commitment as First Lady to promote healthy lifestyles and eating habits among young people, she challenged Girl Scouts to track their exercise and reading habits through the Let's Read, Let's Move initiative.

The New Brownie Elf

As part of the new Girl Scout Leadership Journeys materials introduced in 2008, Girl Scouts reintroduced a beloved character: the Brownie Elf. Popping up in the pages of the Girl Scout Brownie books in the Journeys series, this hip, spunky, updated elf carries on a tradition dating back to the earliest days of Girl Scouting.

SIDEBAR BELOW
Laura Bush and Girl Scouts at the gala celebration of the 90th anniversary of Girl Scouts, Washington, D.C., 2002

SIDEBAR BOTTOM
The Brownie Elf was introduced in 2008.

BOTTOM
Girl Scouts at Space Camp, part of Girl Scout Destinations, 2005

by young people. Facebook, Twitter, and YouTube became tools used daily, if not hourly, accessible via computers, smartphones, and iPads.

And while girls of all ages were blogging, tweeting, texting, and downloading, Girl Scouts was not left behind. New, innovative ways to reach girls—virtually and in real life—made the movement and its principles relevant and necessary in a rapidly changing time. The theme for the Girl Scout membership initiative launched in 2000—"Girl Scouting: For Every Girl, Everywhere"—was a familiar commitment taken to new levels, resulting in membership increases (in 2000, total Girl Scout membership reached 3.7 million, and it surpassed 3.8 million later in the decade).

Throughout the decade leading up to Girl Scouting's 100th anniversary, you could find Girl Scouts scuba diving and exploring marine life in the Florida Keys through the Aquarius Project, traveling to connect with Girl Guides in Thailand, and, through special Girl Scout Wider Opportunities, partaking in such once-in-a-lifetime events as the Antarctic Research Project. Girl Scouts also focused on ways to help others: They donated to hunger relief programs, adopted Ronald McDonald Houses, and assembled birthday celebration kits for needy families for Make a Difference Day. In the aftermath of September 11, 2001, they offered assistance and support to their shell-shocked sisters in New York, Washington, D.C., and Pennsylvania; they held blood drives, hosted remembrance ceremonies, and wrote more than

8,000 thank-you notes to rescue workers. They raised money, collected nonperishable food items, and even sent toys to victims of the 2004 Indian Ocean tsunami and 2005's Hurricane Katrina. The creativity and initiative displayed by individual Girl Scouts and Girl Scout troops put them on the map not only in their own communities but nationally and even internationally, as well.

To stay current with girls in this busy decade, the Girl Scout Research Institute (GSRI) was created in 2000 to conduct research on the healthy development of girls and to educate others about its findings, strengthening Girl Scouts' already established position as a leading authority on girls. Its first initiative, a study titled *Teens Before Their Time*, focused on the increasing pressure for preteens to deal with issues normally faced by girls much older. In 2001, the GSRI conducted a landmark study titled *New Directions for Girls 11-17*. The study's conclusion was a mandate to expand program options offered to older Girl Scouts and to create a Girl Scout experience tailored precisely to their own interests and needs.

An acknowledgment of the importance of flexibility in reaching girls gave rise to the Juliette program in 2001. As a Juliette, a girl could individually register with Girl Scouts without having to join a troop—a good option for girls whose busy schedules didn't allow for full troop participation. Girls could earn awards and recognitions independently and connect with nearby troops for special events and, in some cases, take part in special programs designed for these individually affiliated girls. In addition, at its 2002 National Convention, Girl Scouts introduced STUDIO 2B, an innovative, "girl-centric" program for girls ages 11 to 17. This was a program uniquely created "by girls, for girls," and it provided a new and flexible way to participate in Girl Scouts while still adhering to its core principles. Girls could set their own goals and create their own activities based on their own specific interests and favorite topics. Furthering this endeavor, in 2003, a By Girls, for Girls National Advisory Committee was formed. Composed of Girl Scouts from across the country, it ensured that girls' opinions are always heard.

As more and more girls and their families immigrated to the United States from points south of the border, Girl Scouts intensified its efforts to include them in the movement. A 2002 National Conference on Latinas in Girl Scouting drew wide participation, and new resources were published in Spanish throughout the decade. Mainstream Spanish-language publications, such as *Latina Style* and *Hispanic Times*, began running stories on Girl Scouts and its involvement among their readership. And in March 2004, a targeted Hispanic Initiative partnered Girl Scouts with prominent Hispanic organizations, launched a Spanish-language website, and developed the membership tool kit *Conexiones* to help volunteers and staff better connect with Hispanic communities. And, in 2005, Patricia Diaz Dennis became the first Hispanic woman elected Chair of the National Board of Directors. As a result of

a concerted effort to reach out to Hispanics begun in 2000, membership among Latina girls increased by 63 percent over seven years. Hispanic adult membership increased 57 percent in just two years (2005 to 2007).

During this decade, federal funding made it possible to open new doors and expand Girl Scouts' reach to increasing numbers of girls. In the first decade of the 21st century, Girl Scouts received $11 million in federal funding to reach at-risk girls through initiatives such as Girl Scouts Beyond Bars, Girl Scouts in Detention Centers, and Girl Scouts in Public Housing. Funds made it possible for Girl Scouts to bring a positive, hopeful, forward-looking program to girls in homeless shelters, housing facilities, and women's prisons and helped these girls build their self-esteem, increase their confidence, and turn their lives in a more positive direction. P.A.V.E. the Way (Project Anti-Violence Education), a federally funded violence-prevention project, taught girls conflict resolution, anger management, and personal safety—tools necessary for avoiding or defusing violence before it begins.

In 2000, Girl Scouts celebrated young leaders by recognizing 12 girls at the first annual Girl Scout Gold Award Young Women of Distinction event in Washington, D.C. These very special Senior Girl Scouts were honored for their achievement in the design and implementation of a Girl Scout Gold Award Project, and were treated to meetings with government leaders, workshops in leadership development, and tours of the capital.

"Defy" Ad Campaign

In 2006, Girl Scouts launched an effective and award-winning ad campaign with the theme "Defy." Five taglines appeared on posters and other ad materials, each delivering a strong, positive message for girls: "Defy the Stereotype," "Defy the Ordinary," "Defy Self-Doubt," "Defy Conformity," and "Defy Peer Pressure."

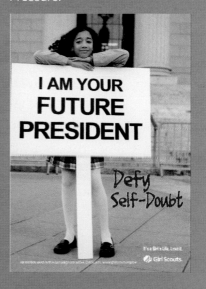

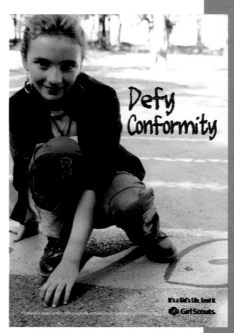

Thin Mint Blizzard

Furthering the notion that there's no combination like Girl Scout Thin Mint cookies and ice cream, Girl Scouts licensed Dairy Queen to create a limited-edition Thin Mint Blizzard in July 2008. The combination was so successful—the Thin Mint Blizzard was the best-selling limited-edition Dairy Queen Blizzard in history, with more than 10 million Blizzards sold in one month—that the promotion was repeated in the summer of 2009, and the Tagalongs Peanut Butter Patties Blizzard was also introduced that season. As a bonus, Dairy Queen's accompanying series of clever TV ads presented Girl Scouts as fun, smart, and business savvy.

SIDEBAR
Dairy Queen Thin Mint Blizzard and Tagalongs Blizzard advertisements

The annual practice of honoring girls that began in 2000 was followed in 2002 with a 90th-anniversary gala event on March 12 in the Great Hall of the Building Museum in Washington, D.C. There, the movement celebrated Girl Scouts' Women of Distinction—10 nationally renowned women leaders, including fashion designer Vera Wang; Alma J. Powell, chair of America's Promise—The Alliance for Youth; Elizabeth Dole, former U.S. senator and president of the American Red Cross; and astronaut Kathryn Sullivan, Ph.D. Also available at the event were copies of the book *Every Girl Tells a Story: A Celebration of Girls Speaking Their Minds*, a collaboration between Girl Scouts of the USA and photographer Carolyn Jones that featured first-person accounts of girls ages 12 to 18 who overcame adversity. On the following day, the first Congressional Lobby Day, nearly 350 Girl Scout representatives met with members of Congress to educate them about the needs of youth in their communities and the important work of the Girl Scout councils in reaching an ever-increasing number of girls.

The well-intentioned efforts of the early 2000s covered new ground—reaching a more diverse population and setting a good direction—but they weren't enough to satisfy a growing concern about the gap between Girl Scouts' relevance and value and its perception among the general public. Membership began to fade, owing to outdated programs and volunteer systems that were too cumbersome, and Girl Scouts' strong brand was not holding up as it

once had. Girl Scout councils, the tried and true local delivery arm of Girl Scouting, were not universally strong, and some were too small to work effectively in an increasingly complex world.

Kathy Cloninger, newly hired as National CEO near the end of 2003, was the first to publicly acknowledge these truths and set a strong and clear course toward the future. Cloninger—and everyone involved in Girl Scouting—was determined to find a way to be relevant to girls today yet remain true to the essence, principles, and values of the movement. Emulating the style and determination of Juliette Low, Girl Scout staff and volunteers from around the country gathered together to answer this question: What does Girl Scouts do better than anyone else in the world? The answer was *leadership*. With that clarity of direction, Girl Scouts launched on a path to become the premier leadership experience for girls in the United States.

Girl Scout Groovy Girls

In 2007, Girl Scouts licensed the Manhattan Toy company the rights to manufacture Girl Scout dolls under its popular Groovy Girls brand of soft fabric dolls. The Troop Groovy Girls line of dolls represented the diverse ethnic backgrounds of Girl Scouts themselves and were given names reflecting the values of the Girl Scout Law: Honest Hala, Caring Caitlin, Respectful Roxi, Courageous Camara, and Friendly Fionna, to name a few. The dolls were dressed in the signature fun fashion of Groovy Girls and also wore Girl Scout sashes. Additional accessories, like camping gear, were available, too.

Not only did Groovy Girls advance the Girl Scout brand, but they were excellent toys as well. The Troop Groovy Girls line was named the Toy Industry Association's 2008 Girl Toy of the Year and received a positive mention in the June 2007 issue of *Parents* magazine. Best of all, perhaps, was the impact the dolls had on the girls who received them. One mom wrote Manhattan Toy to thank the company for the quality and integrity of the Groovy Girls line, as well as to tell how the Troop Groovy Girls dolls inspired her five-year-old daughter to become a Girl Scout Daisy herself!

Look What a Cookie Can Do

Since Girl Scout cookie sales began in earnest in the 1920s, the humble Girl Scout cookie has gone from a home-baked money-earner to the object of the largest girl-run business in the world. In the few months that Girl Scout cookies are sold each year, they generate more than $700 million in sales and engage the business skills of girls of all ages, from Girl Scout Daisies on up.

Proceeds from Girl Scout cookie sales always benefit the local troop selling the cookies, but beyond that, the sales help shape the leaders of tomorrow in a manner consistent with the contemporary mission of Girl Scouts. The girls involved develop skills in goal setting, decision making, money management, working with people, and business ethics. An important first experience with entrepreneurship as well as everyday budgeting, Girl Scout cookie sales give girls business leadership skills no matter what they grow up to become—whether heads of corporations, heads of households, or both.

The foundation of change was the Core Business Strategy, an integrated plan to reinvigorate the Girl Scout movement nationwide. With the help of Columbia Business School professor Willie Pietersen, Girl Scouts defined its priorities for this transformation: creating a new outcomes-based program model, developing options for volunteer engagement and girl affiliation, reinvigorating the brand, creating an efficient and effective organizational structure, and substantially increasing funding. A new mission statement, proudly proclaiming that "Girl Scouts builds girls of courage, confidence, and character who make the world a better place," was proposed and embraced

with overwhelming support at the National Council Session in Atlanta in October 2005.

In 2005 and through the remainder of the decade, Cloninger, in close partnership with the National Board, led the movement in a historic transformation through implementation of the Core Business Strategy. Both exciting and challenging, this new strategy was unprecedented in its scope and in the timeliness of its execution. The council restructuring, redesign of Girl Scout program activities, and stewardship of resources advanced councils and enabled Girl Scouts to better meet the needs of girls in the 21st century.

Work on the transformation included extensive research on all aspects of the movement, leading to the creation of a leadership-development program called the Girl Scout Leadership Experience, which became the foundation for all work with girls. The model was based on 15 national leadership outcomes, making it possible, for the first time since the organization was founded, for the organization to quantify the positive effect it has had on members. To create more efficient and effective councils, boundaries were reorganized, reducing the number of councils from 315 to 112. Pathway models were developed for pilot testing to give girls ways to belong to Girl Scouts other than the traditional troop model. A new brand campaign with the tagline "What did you do today?" was launched as an initial step in creating a compelling and contemporary brand. A new initiative to license the Girl Scout brand to many

Uniforms

In conjunction with the 2000 launch of the new Handbook, Badge Book, and Try-it book, Girl Scouts updated the formal dress uniform to include clothing inspired by casual sportswear, including sweatshirts, T-shirts, and cargo pants. Comfortable, practical, and fashionable, they were a far cry from the tailored dresses and sharp ensembles of decades past.

In 2006, the National Board adopted a new formal dress code, which, for the first time, made it a requirement to wear the formal dress uniform when participating in a Girl Scout ceremony or when representing the organization in public. Girls were given the flexibility to wear their own white shirts and khaki pants or skirts along with their official sashes or vests to display their hard-earned awards. For official occasions, adults were required to wear navy blue business attire with a Girl Scout scarf and membership pin.

To illustrate just how far uniforms had come during nearly a century of Girl Scouting, Girl Scouts in 2000 published *The Cut of the Cloth: A Brief History of the Girl Scout Uniform from 1912 to 1999*, a fun retrospective of Girl Scout gear from the movement's beginnings.

Patricia Diaz Dennis

In October 2005, Patricia Diaz Dennis was elected National President. She was the first Hispanic woman to hold the position. She had previously held office as National Secretary (1999–2002) and First Vice President (2002–2005). A resident of San Antonio, Texas, this former girl member is a three-time presidential appointee. She has served in the State Department, on the Federal Communications Commission, and on the National Labor Relations Board.

SIDEBAR
Patricia Diaz Dennis, circa 2005

OPPOSITE
A group visits the White House as President Barack Obama signs the Girl Scouts of the USA Commemorative Coin Act and First Lady Michelle Obama looks on, 2009.

different consumer products was another way Girls Scouts was able to expand brand awareness and cast Girl Scouts in a contemporary light.

To take full advantage of the new program, age groupings were changed to reflect grade level rather than age, ensuring that girls would be grouped with social and developmental peers, maximizing their educational opportunities and, most important, fun. A new level was also created—that of Girl Scout Ambassador—for girls in grades 11 and 12.

Girl Scout Leadership Journeys were developed for all age levels. Focusing on contemporary themes and tied to the 15 national outcomes, these journeys help girls learn about their world and themselves while guiding them to take action to make the world a better place. The first Leadership Journey was released in 2008 with the theme "It's Your World—Change It!" It consisted of 12 books (a girl book and accompanying adult guide for each grade level) on the theme of advocacy. In 2009, Girl Scouts released another Leadership Journey, featuring an environmental theme, called "It's Your Planet—Love It!" A third Leadership Journey, focusing on creative expression and called "It's Your Story—Tell It!" was released in 2010.

Core program subjects, such as environmental action, healthy living, financial literacy, Global Girl Scouting, and STEM (Science, Technology, Engineering, and Math), continued to be offered, with a new emphasis on helping girls learn to act as leaders within those areas.

In 2011, the iconic Girl Scout handbooks and badge books were updated in time for the kickoff of Girl Scouts' 100th-anniversary year.

The badge activities were revamped to be more relevant to 21st-century girls and included badges on up-to-the-minute topics such as Innovation, Digital Arts, and Science and Technology.

In addition, seven Legacy badge categories were created to focus on topics that had been part of Girl Scouts since the very beginning. The badges offered in these categories—Artist, Athlete, Citizen, Cook, First Aid, Girl Scout Way, and Naturalist—honored the past while refreshing activities to keep them current.

Amid the high-energy work of transformation, Girl Scouts took time to celebrate the accomplishments of the decade, including the 75th anniversary of "Macy Magic" at the Edith Macy Conference Center in 2001, the 90th anniversary of the Girl Scout Cookie Program in 2007, and the 95th anniversary of Girl Scouting in 2007, as well. The 50th anniversary of the Juliette Gordon Low Birthplace in Savannah was celebrated in 2006, for which the

Birthplace underwent a restoration including the repair of its staircase, the installation of an elevator to improve accessibility, and the restoration of many rooms to their 1886 appearance. And on October 29, 2009, just two days before the birthday of Juliette Low, President Barack Obama signed the Girl Scouts of the USA Commemorative Coin Act, authorizing a special Girl Scouts coin to be minted in 2013, one of only two commemorative coins scheduled for that year.

As Girl Scouts celebrates its 100th anniversary, its next century rolls out before it like a blank scroll, inviting the next chapter of Girl Scout history to be written. It's impossible to tell what the next hundred years of Girl Scouts will bring, but we can be sure of a few things: The Girl Scout movement will continue to find the best ways to reach girls—whoever and wherever they may be—in the most accessible and relevant ways possible. It will continue to take up the challenges the nation and the world will present to it. And it will continue to absolutely bubble over with that hopeful, irrepressible energy of girls.

Girl Scout Leadership Journeys

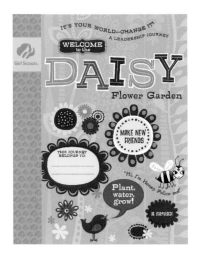

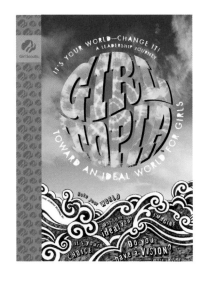

As Girl Scouting heads toward its 100th anniversary, girls at each grade level have three journeys to help them develop their leadership skills.

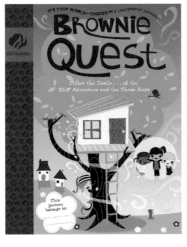

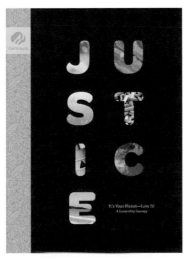

The Girl's Guide to Girl Scouting

Girl Scout Daisies earn ten petals (one for each line of the Girl Scout Law), plus Financial Literacy and Cookie Business leaves.

A sampling of Brownie badges. From left: Pets, My Family Story, Letterboxer, Dancer

A sampling of Junior badges. From left: Jeweler, Scribe, Social Butterfly, Musician

The iconic Girl Scout badge books and handbooks were reimagined and released in 2011, just in time for the kickoff of Girl Scouts' 100th anniversary. Some badge categories reflected topics that have been important to Girl Scouts since 1912, such as Outdoors, First Aid, Cook, and Citizen. Other badge categories—such as Digital Arts, Innovation, and Investigation—were created to match the interests of 21st-century girls. In addition, new Financial Literacy and Cookie Business badges were created for girls at all grade levels.

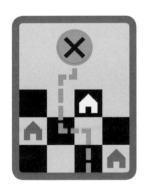

A sampling of Cadette badges. From left: Science of Happiness, Digital Movie Maker, Entrepreneur, Trees

A sampling of Senior badges. From left: Game Visionary, Sky, Troupe Performer, Locavore

A sampling of Ambassador badges. From left: Photography, Public Policy, Dinner Party, Water

The Girl's Guide to Girl Scouting also offered Financial Literacy and Cookie Business badges for each year of Girl Scouting.

What Did You Do Today?

In 2010, Girl Scouts of the USA launched a multifaceted brand refresh in preparation for the 100th anniversary of Girl Scouting. Under the theme "What Did You Do Today?" Girl Scouts shone a spotlight on the wonderfully adventurous things Girl Scouts were doing with their days, while illustrating the Girl Scout values of leadership, sisterhood, and inclusion. Most important, Girl Scouts wanted to clearly communicate its brand promise: Girl Scouts gives every girl access to life-changing experiences that inspire her to do something big.

Wildlife Rescue   Self Defense   Whitewater Rafting   Robotics Research
X-Camp   Explore Europe   Photography   Entrepreneurship
Museum Sleepovers   Habitat Homes   Space Camp   Consult At The UN

WHAT DID YOU DO TODAY?

girl scouts 2011

You can change the world. Girl Scouts can give you the opportunities and the tools. And you can get started right here and now, in your own backyard. Learn more at girlscouts.org/today.

Entrepreneurship   Habitat Homes   Museum Sleepovers   Consult At The UN
Robotics Research   Advocate For Change   Explore Europe   Wildlife Rescue
Whitewater Rafting   Photojournalism   Self Defense   Space Camp

REGISTER TO VOTE

WHAT DID YOU DO TODAY?

girl scouts 2011

Have a voice. Take a stand. You can make a difference, and we can help you get started with opportunities ranging from around the corner to around the world. Visit girlscouts.org/today to learn more.

Girl Scouts of the USA
National Headquarters
420 Fifth Avenue
New York, NY 10018-2798
212-852-5000

Girl Scouts of the USA
Public Policy and Advocacy Office
816 Connecticut Avenue, NW
Third Floor
Washington, DC 20006
advocacy@girlscouts.org

Juliette Gordon Low Birthplace,
Girl Scout National Center
10 East Oglethorpe Avenue
Savannah, GA 31401
(912) 233-4501
www.juliettegordonlowbirthplace.org
birthplace@girlscouts.org

Edith Macy Conference Center
550 Chappaqua Road
Briarcliff Manor, NY 10510
914.945.8000
www.edithmacy.com
macysales@benchmarkmanagement.com

To learn more about the Girl Scout
organization and how today's Girl Scouts
are making the world a better place, go to:
www.girlscouts.org

To find a council near you,
go to: www.girlscouts.org/councilfinder/

To learn more about the Girl Scout
Alumnae Association, go to: http://
alumnae.girlscouts.org

To learn more about the Girl Scout Research
Institute, go to: www.girlscouts.org/research

To learn more about the Girl Scout National
Historic Preservation Center and Girl Scout
history, go to: www.girlscouts.org/who_we_
are/history/

National Presidents

June 1915	Juliette Gordon Low
January 1920	Anne Hyde Choate
January 1922	Lou Henry Hoover
May 1925	Dean Sarah Louise Arnold
October 1928	Mira H. Hoffman
October 1930	Birdsall Otis Edey
October 1935	Lou Henry Hoover
October 1937	Henrietta Bates Brooke
October 1939	Mildred E. Mudd
October 1941	Helen H. Means
March 1946	Harriet R. Ferguson
October 1951	Olivia Layton
November 1957	Marjorie M. Culmer
October 1963	Margaret W. Price
October 1969	Grace M. S. MacNeil
October 1972	Marjorie Ittman
October 1975	Dr. Gloria D. Scott
October 1978	Jane C. Freeman
October 1984	Betty F. Pilsbury
October 1990	B. LaRae Orullian
October 1996	Elinor Johnstone Ferdon
October 1999	Connie L. Matsui
October 2002	Cynthia Bramlett Thompson
October 2005	Patricia Diaz Dennis
October 2008	Connie L. Lindsey

National Honorary Presidents

October 1917	Edith B. Wilson
March 1921	Florence K. Harding
January 1924	Grace Coolidge
November 1929	Lou Henry Hoover
March 1933	Eleanor Roosevelt
May 1945	Bess Truman
February 1953	Mamie Eisenhower
January 1961	Jacqueline Kennedy
December 1963	Lady Bird Johnson
February 1969	Pat Nixon
August 1976	Betty Ford
March 1977	Rosalynn Carter
May 1981	Nancy Reagan
June 1989	Barbara Bush
February 1993	Hillary Rodham Clinton
June 2001	Laura Bush
October 2009	Michelle Obama

Chief Executive Officers

6/13–2/14	Edith Johnston	National Secretary
2/14–6/16	Cora Neal	National Secretary
6/16–8/17	Montague Gammon	National Secretary
8/17–1/19	Abby Porter Leland	National Director
2/19–6/30	Jane Deeter Rippin	National Director
6/30–11/30	Emma H. Gunther	Acting Director
11/30–9/35	Josephine Schain	National Director
9/35–12/50	Constance Rittenhouse	National Director
1/51–6/60	Dorothy C. Stratton,	National Executive Director
7/60–5/61	Sally Stickney Cortner	Interim NED
6/61–2/72	Louise A. Wood,	National Executive Director
4/72–8/75	Dr. Cecily C. Selby,	National Executive Director
8/75–7/76	Frank H. Kanis	Interim NED
7/76–1/90	Frances R. Hesselbein,	National Executive Director
2/90–10/97	Mary Rose Main,	National Executive Director
11/97–2/98	Joel E. Becker	Interim NED
2/98–7/02	Marsha Johnson Evans,	National Executive Director
7/02–10/03	Jackie Barnes	Interim NED/CEO
10/03–	Kathy Cloninger	CEO

Acknowledgments

Connie L. Lindsey
Chair, National Board of Directors

Kathy Cloninger
Chief Executive Officer

Florence Corsello
Senior Vice President and Chief
Financial Officer, Business Services

Timothy Higdon
Chief of External Affairs

Jaclyn E. Libowitz
Chief of Staff

Jan A. Verhage
Chief Operating Officer

Deborah Long
Senior Vice President, Governance
and Corporate Administration

Laurel J. Richie
Senior Vice President and
Chief Marketing Officer

Laurie A. Westley
Senior Vice President, Public Policy,
Advocacy, and the Research Institute

Michael Watson
Senior Vice President,
Human Resources

Special thanks to: Kelly Amabile, Doug Bantz, Alex Barnes, Gail Benson, Bettye Bradley, Karen Bremberg, Valerie Brennan, Clare Bresnahan, Gerri Brown, Joseph Bush, Kelly Chatman, Brian Crawford, Kaylee Davis, Eileen Doyle, Laura Edlin, Martha Foley, Girl Scout History Volunteers, Karina Gee, Yevgeniya Gribov, Fran Powell Harold, Suzanne Harper, Barry Horowitz, Amanda Hudson, Katherine Knapp Keena, Ken Kirschner, Heather Lawrence, Alisha Niehaus, Melvin Ortiz, Jenn Pelly, Rodney Roman, Michal Spelda, Michelle Tompkins, and Gil Vidal.

Index

Page numbers in *italics* refer to illustrations

Photo Credits

Photographs and other images are from the collections of the Girl Scout National Historic Preservation Center and Juliette Gordon Low Birthplace, a Girl Scout National Center, except where noted. Page 68: photo of Dagmar Wright, Girl Scout Golden Eaglet, gift of Dagmar (Wright) Yablsey, used by permission. Page 68: photo of Kathleen Kelly, Girl Scout Golden Eaglet, gift of Kathleen (Kelly) Boettigheimer, used by permission. Page 71: scrapbook of Jerrene Lucas, Girl Scout Golden Eaglet, donated by Laura Pittman. Page 75: photo of Babe Ruth—The MLB Trademarks depicted were licensed by MLBP, Inc. Page 94: WAGGGS World Badge and logo used by permission of World Association of Girl Guides and Girl Scouts. Page 155: Juliette Gordon Low portrait by Edward Hughes used by permission of National Portrait Gallery, Smithsonian Institution/Art Resource, NY. Page 207: Dairy Queen Thin Mint Cookie Blizzard Treat and Tagalongs Peanut Butter Patties Blizzard Treat images used by permission of American Dairy Queen Corp. Page 207: Troop Groovy Girls image used by permission of Manhattan Toy.

About the author

Betty Christiansen is the author of *Knitting for Peace* (STC Craft). She has an MFA in nonfiction writing from Sarah Lawrence College and lives with her family in La Crosse, Wisconsin, where she is the editor of the regional women's magazine *Coulee Region Women*.

Published in 2011 by Stewart, Tabori & Chang
An imprint of ABRAMS

Copyright © 2011 Girl Scouts of the USA. All Rights Reserved. The GIRL SCOUTS® name, mark and all associated trademarks and logotypes, including the Trefoil Design, are owned by Girl Scouts of the USA. Stewart, Tabori & Chang, a division of Harry N. Abrams, Inc., is an official GSUSA licensed vendor.
www.girlscouts.org

All rights reserved. No portion of this book may be reproduced, stored in a retrieval system, or transmitted in any form or by any means, mechanical, electronic, photocopying, recording, or otherwise, without written permission from the publisher.

Cataloging-in-Publication Data has been applied for and may be obtained from the Library of Congress.
ISBN: 978-1-58479-942-9

Editor: Jennifer Levesque
Designer: Darilyn Lowe Carnes
Production Manager: Anet Sirna-Bruder

The text of this book was composed in Archer and Omnes.

Printed and bound in U.S.A.
10 9 8 7 6 5 4 3 2 1

Stewart, Tabori & Chang books are available at special discounts when purchased in quantity for premiums and promotions as well as fundraising or educational use. Special editions can also be created to specification. For details, contact specialsales@abramsbooks.com or the address below.

THE ART OF BOOKS SINCE 1949
115 West 18th Street
New York, NY 10011
www.abramsbooks.com

FRONT COVER

Art from the collection of the Girl Scout National Historic Preservation Center. "Campward Ho!" Girl Scout silhouette from *The American Girl*, July 1930.

BACK COVER

Art from the collection of the Girl Scout National Historic Preservation Center. Girl Scout drawing from the cover of the first Girl Scout Handbook, *How Girls Can Help Their Country*, published in 1913.

FRONTISPIECE

All images are from the collection of the Girl Scout National Historic Preservation Center, except where noted. Clockwise from top left: *Girl Scout Equipment* catalog, 1937; *Girl Scout Songbook*, 1929; Girl Scout postcard "The Golden Ground," by Edith Ballinger Price, 1933; Girl Scout uniform belt with whistle, knife, and purse, 1928–1936; Girl Scout uniform neckerchief, early 1920s; uniform sleeve with proficiency badges of Girl Scout Golden Eaglet and Mariner Dagmar Wright, 1930s (gift of Dagmar [Wright] Yablsey); *Who Are the Girl Scouts* booklet, 1934; Girl Scout card game *Trupe*, 1939; playing cards from *Trupe*, 1939; Girl Scout postcard "The Golden Hand," by Edith Ballinger Price, 1933; Silver Anniversary Dinner of the Girl Scouts 1912–1937 program and menu, 1937; *Twenty-five Years of Girl Scouting: 1912–1937*, by Katharine O. Wright, 1937; *Girl Scout Proficiency Badge Requirements and Special Awards*, 1934; Girl Scout equipment collapsible drinking cup, 1930s; Girl Scout Intermediate proficiency badges, 1938–1963: Junior Citizen, Scholarship, Housekeeper; Girl Scouts annual report, 1933.

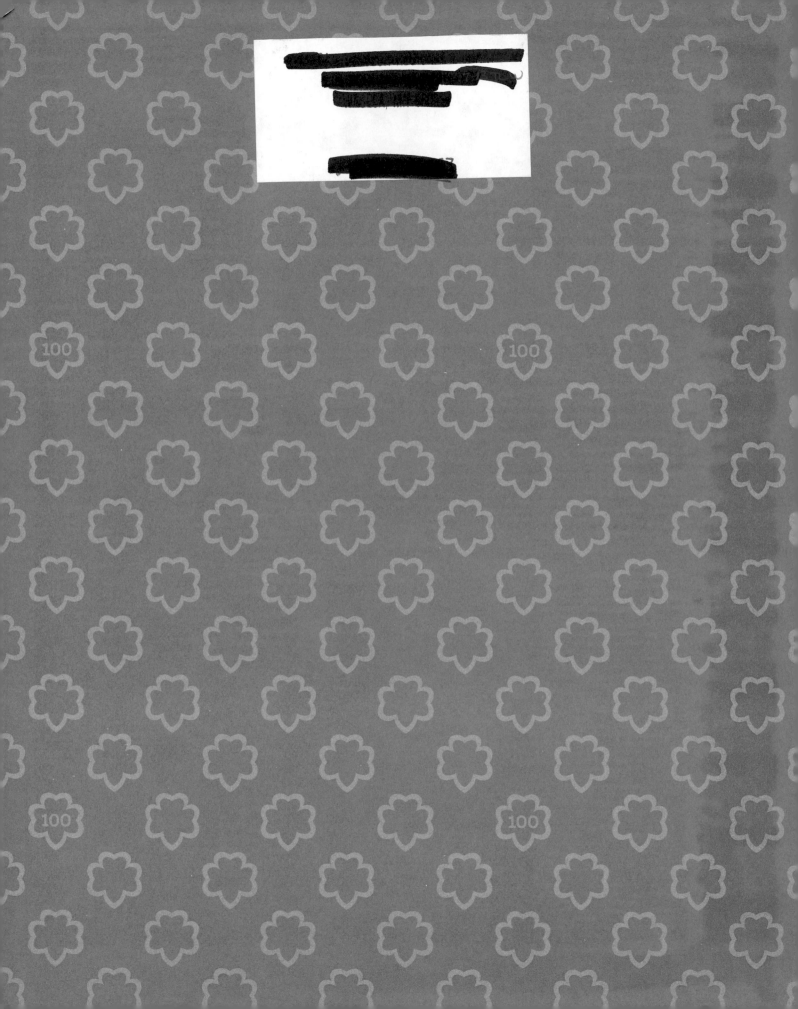